In *Search* of a *Unicorn*

(Or, Dismounting from a Three-Horned Dilemma)

By Tommy Downs

Order this book online at www.trafford.com
or email orders@trafford.com

Most Trafford titles are also available at major online book retailers.

© Copyright 2010 Tommy Downs.

All rights reserved. No part of this publication may be reproduced, stored in a retrieval system, or transmitted, in any form or by any means, electronic, mechanical, photocopying, recording, or otherwise, without the written prior permission of the author.

Printed in Victoria, BC, Canada.

ISBN: 978-1-4251-3455-6 (sc)
ISBN: 978-1-4251-3456-3 (e)

Our mission is to efficiently provide the world's finest, most comprehensive book publishing service, enabling every author to experience success. To find out how to publish your book, your way, and have it available worldwide, visit us online at www.trafford.com

Trafford rev. 1/27/2010

www.trafford.com

North America & international
toll-free: 1 888 232 4444 (USA & Canada)
phone: 250 383 6864 ♦ fax: 812 355 4082

# # # # #

An episodic and anecdotal account of some of the attempts to restore the church as it existed in New Testament times as I have personally researched, witnessed, and experienced some of those attempts.

# # # # #

Horn 1
The Christian Church (Disciples of Christ)

Horn 2
The Christian Churches - Churches of Christ

Horn 3
The churches of Christ

Miscellaneous bumps and warts that may pass as horns

The Unicorn?
"My" church of Matthew 16:18

Dedicated to Mervin, a disciple, a Christian and a member of the church of Christ.

Table of Contents

	Preface	Page vii
1	In the Beginning	Page 19
2	The Quarterly Supper	Page 48
3	Close(d) Communion	Page 69
4	The Small "C" Church	Page 83
5	From Sunday School to Church Member	Page 89
6	A Start at Preaching	Page 105
7	Four More Years in Texas	Page 151
8	Another Christian Church Preacher	Page 187
9	Quintessentially Independent	Page 202
10	Mexico or Mississippi?	Page 253
11	Teaching Without Classes	Page 271
12	Sixty-Three Souls in Brownlee	Page 282
13	Mennonites and Methodists	Page 291
14	Free From What?	Page 306
15	Where the Buffalos Roam	Page 314
16	Men of "The Word"	Page 329

The Appendices

A	A Communion Meditation.	(Poem)	Page 346
B	Things Not Meant to Be .	(Poem)	Page 348
C	A Christmas Prayer	(Poem)	Page 351
D	My Philosophy of Education.	(Essay)	Page 359
E	Two Peas in a Pod	(Short Story)	Page 378
F	An Alphabet of Churches	(Listing)	Page 401
G	Some Men Who Tried	(Listing)	Page 411
H	The Gospel According to Gimpy	(Short Story)	Page 417
I	O'Kelly's Plan of Union	(Essay)	Page 429
J	The Promise	(Short Story)	Page 442
K	The Silver Trombone	(Short Story)	Page 462
L	The Question Mark Mind	(Poem)	Page 486
M	Butcher	(Short Story)	Page 493
N	Macedonia	(Historical)	Page 503
O	The Meanings of "EIS"	(Listing)	Page 508

Preface

Most of this book explains itself—at least insofar as an explanation is needed or is possible. Frankly, there may be some parts that defy explanation! I did not mean for it to be that way. However as I was writing and really got going, some things seem to have just snuck in.

The word "snuck" is not one of those things. I just consulted my trusty little computer dictionary which is always on the desktop with its red icon always at hand! I therefore can guarantee you that *snuck* is truly a word.

Several idiosyncrasies of language may have to be explained as we go along. There are some words that I just won't use. Want an example?

Well, I never use the word "church" to refer to a building (unless it is part of a name or unless it is necessary for clarity—or unless I goof up and do it accidentally) even though I am aware that most dictionaries will give "a building" as the first meaning of the word.

I remember when I tried to make a living selling encyclopedias that one of the selling points for the edition I was selling was its simplicity—a boon for selling to parents and kids. The specific reference that the trainers-of-the-salesmen suggested that we use was the word *bird*, a monstrosity of a definition in most encyclopedias and dictionaries, including my Oxford and my little handy-dandy computer dictionary with its bright red icon always-on-the-desktop. Here is what it says: bird (bÙrd)   n. any of a class (Aves) of warmblooded, two-legged, egg-laying vertebrates with feathers and wings [and so on, for eight definitions.]

Tommy Downs

The encyclopedia I was selling began simply with "bird: an animal with feathers" and then went on with more information for people who needed more information--but simple words at the beginning for the kids who did not need any more gobbledygook.

But back to the subject at hand! I was talking about using the word CHURCH only in its true, New Testament-inspired meaning, not in the meaning usually given first in the dictionary. Look how far down the list in this typical dictionary entry we must go to find that the church is *people!*

- a building set apart or consecrated for public worship, esp. one for Christian worship
- religious service or public worship, esp. among Christians
- all Christians considered as a single body

- a particular sect or denomination of Christians
- the ecclesiastical government of a particular religious group as opposed to secular government
- the profession of the clergy; clerical profession
- a group of worshipers; congregation

I find it more appropriate to use the word congregation or the word assembly when I am referring to a local group of Christians, especially when I am talking or writing to people not familiar with the Christian patois.

(Teaser Question: Do you go to *church* on Sundays?)

I started writing these "introductory comments," which I have now more properly labeled *preface* (written by the author himself, as opposed to a *foreword* which is usually written by someone other than the author) in order to explain about my INTERLUDES that you were supposed to come across from time to time. Maybe you will get bored or tired of reading the particular subject matter you are reading and need a change of pace—so I decided to provide you with some "interludes." (My real purpose was to introduce you to some materials that just doesn't seem to fit anywhere else!) and somewhere along the way when I was writing about Quill Lake, I decided I would like for you to read "Two Peas in a Pod," a short story I was inspired[1] to write because of an incident that occurred in that village. *[Appendix E]* Or when Regina Avenue

---

[1] *I do not mean "inspired" in a "from God" sense!*

Christian Church (that is its *name*) decided to do something different: they called a minister from the United Church of Canada (and again the word "Church" because that is its name!) That unusual situation prompted me to write "The Gospel According to Gimpy" *[Appendix H]* and that doesn't really fit into the search for a unicorn—so I was going to provide it as an interlude. The same goes for "A Communion Meditation," which I hope will provide you with some special thoughts. *[Appendix A]*

My little dictionary says that an interlude is a short, humourous play formerly presented between the parts of a miracle play or morality play or a short play of a sort popular in the Tudor period, either farcical or moralistic in tone and with a plot typically derived from French farce or the morality play or any performance between the acts of a play, or instrumental music played between the parts of a song, liturgy, play, etc. (Whew!) Well, my use of the word would have been the last one listed in my dictionary: a) anything that fills time between two events b) intervening time or, rarely, space.

But letting someone read my manuscript in its early stages obliterated all those interludes! You can still read them—but not as interludes. Now you will find a reference to them in the body of the book, but you will have to go to an appendix to find what would have been an interlude.

I hope that you will find some

enjoyment or some inspiration in at least one of those would-be interludes that I have included—in an appendix!

Another point I want to make in these introductory comments concerns people. People are important. People are the church and the church is people. Consider this: one of my favourite adages (which I think I originated in this particular form which, then, by definition makes it not an adage because an adage is old, but here it is):

> God is LOVE.
> JESUS is God.
> The CHURCH is the body of Christ
> We are the CHURCH.
> Therefore we <u>must</u> LOVE!

One of the "fathers" of the Stone-

Campbell (Restoration) Movement was a man named Peter Ainslie III. It is said about him that when he encountered Christians who were lax in showing love, he commented, "They are my people and I love them, but they sure can bungle things up, can't they?"

That leads me to say that the people I write about are real. I have used real names of real people. I truly believe that I have learned something from every person whom it has been my honour and privilege to be acquainted with—especially Christian persons. I therefore want to give their names—not just "a person" or "a man I know". You see, in my first draft that is what I did. I was writing about "a lady" who worked so hard on the constitution for the

In Search of a Unicorn

Regina Avenue Christian Church when suddenly it occurred to me that she had a name and I knew her name so why was I just calling her "a lady?" So I had to go back and do a re-write: it was Cody Harvey who did such a good job on the constitution.

Perhaps you will find your name here somewhere—or the name of someone you know. I hope so.

And I believe you will—because we Christians have a way of sharing our friends, don't we?

Chapter One

IN THE BEGINNING

Sunday after Sunday in the early thirties I went to Sunday School and I usually "stayed for church" at the (Southern) Baptist church in the town of Brandon, Mississippi, where I was born. Brandon was a little town then, less than five hundred or so people, probably fewer. Brandon was and still is the county seat of Rankin County, a county established by the Legislature of the State of Mississippi, in 1928, the same year that I was born. The stores and other businesses (a bank, a newspaper office, an insurance broker, a barber shop, etc.) along with the county court house all surrounded a uniquely-designed town square--grassy and well-landscaped--where a lofty, battle-equipped Confederate soldier made of bronze stood his stolid guard on his solid concrete pedestal.

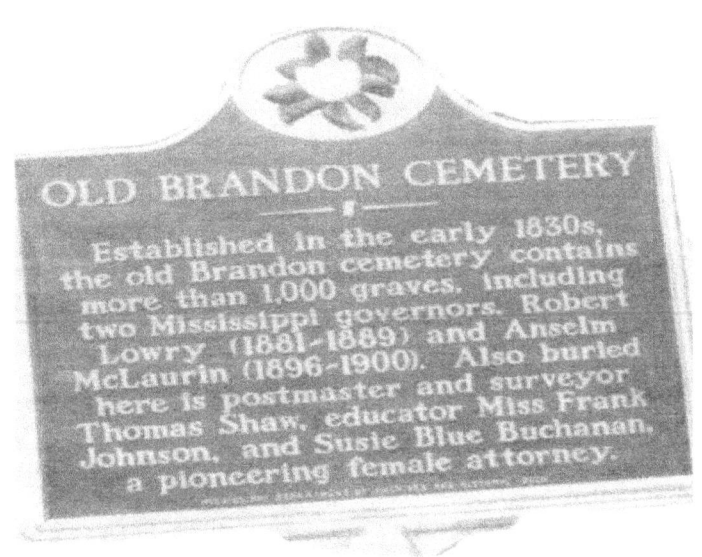

Tommy Downs

Whatever the weather, I walked to Sunday School and "church", past the *always* freshly-painted, frame building labeled Methodist church which was next door to our house on one side. The town cemetery was our neighbour on the other side.

On Sunday night, June 1, 2008, I parked my small RV that some call a camper or a van, but at the price I paid for it, I use its proper nomenclature—a Class B motor home in the driveway of the house I was born in—right next to the cemetery gate! I spent the night there—eighty years after I was born in that house. I also found that today the AME church is the Baptist Church of the Living Water, or something like that. Many years after we had moved away, though Mama still owned the house and lot, the cemetery was enlarged by about a half-acre or more by the process of *eminent domain.* Some friends told my mother that she should not be concerned that they had taken her land without her permission, because now all the coffins and vaults, etc. that had been buried there belonged to her!

After the cemetery, the town was no more. There was just the hilly, wooded, countryside for a couple of miles, down a long, long hill--a gravelled road all the way until one reached the little community called ***Value***. Value was the point along the railway that was the location of the railroad station that served Brandon, with the railroad going on to Jackson, Vicksburg, Shreveport, etc., then on to Dallas and points west and in the other direction, east to Meridian, Birmingham, Atlanta--and on up to Washington and New York and Boston, if that was your desire.

I never quite learned why the Brandon railway station was two or three miles away in a place with a completely different and seemingly unrelated name, but I was only a kid: what did I know? Anyhow, I moved away from Brandon when I was nine!

Except for special occasions, the only people who attended the Methodist church next door to our house were black people, though these days (AD 2008) the acceptable term for them is African-American. Today I know the church *was* an AME Church (African Methodist Episcopal). In those days they were politely referred to as Negroes and impolitely referred to by what has come to be known as "the N-word." I do not ever recall hearing my parents use that particular word nor did I very often hear it amongst any of my family, though the slurred way of saying "Negro" often came out "Nigra". (Could my father's Indiana boyhood have anything to do with that, I wonder?)

Though he was born in Bell County, Texas, my father grew up in Indiana, in or near Terre Haute. I do not know how long he lived there--and none of his siblings is still alive for me to question. It must have been a long time for his mother, though, because she always seemed to me to have an accent that we Southerners referred to as

"Yankee". I would even say that my daddy's speech was slightly "Yankee-fied," too. At least it was quite different from my mama's pure Southern drawl. An example of *her* special patois was her pronunciation of the word "onion" which almost defied analysis. I am certain that no other person on earth ever said it the same way! I will try to indicate her sounds: ***earn-gin.*** Not like a cotton gin nor gin that some folks drink, but with the second syllable rhyming with the second syllable of "again," a hard *g* I guess it is called.

You know, it never really occurred to me then that there was anything strange about walking past *that* church building next door to our house and traveling almost completely across the town. (And it was a long way across town: the town limits circled that soldier in the square at exactly a one-mile radius. So to get to "our" church, since I lived right at the edge of town except for the cemetery, I had a long walk.) In addition to the AME Church, I walked past the

Episcopal church building (for you Canadians, that's the American equivalent of the Anglicans) and the Presbyterian church building before I ever got to the building known then as the Brandon Baptist Church where a group of Southern Baptists met for worship, a group now known as First Baptist Church of Brandon. I suppose the "First" got added to the name when, as time went by, it became evident that other "kinds" of Baptists were going to be building and working in Brandon. And true to expectations, it is now possible to find those others in the town--though it is no longer a little town, but a fairly large suburb, along with Pearl and a host of other former little towns, a vital part of the Metro-Jackson metropolis. (And true to Baptist tradition and heritage, the "First" designation is necessary to differentiate this congregation from those that have split off and perhaps otherwise have formed new congregations.)

Off to the southeast of downtown

there was a beautiful, imposing red brick building with bright white wooden trim where the *white* Methodists worshipped. Scattered somewhere around town there must have been two or three or four other places of worship since I remember as a child hearing of the "holy rollers" and Pentecostals and a few other groups. But we went to Sunday School and almost always "stayed for church" at the Baptist church building.

My daddy and my mama and my brothers and my sisters were all there, including one brother who did not live at home. He was about six years older than I was, and for reasons of health (I was told, though he never appeared to me to be anything but the picture of health!) he lived out in the country about six or eight miles from town with my maternal grandparents, affectionately known as "Daddy Wynn and Mammy". The country living must have done some good: my two other, older brothers and my older sister have all died at the time of this writing (autumn of 2006), but the "sickly" one who lived with my grandparents is still living and is in his late eighties--with a pace-maker (which he keeps "tuned up" by holding a telephone receiver to his side and phoning his doctor's office!) and some other problems with his heart, but still enjoying life in the country just a mile or so from where he lived as a boy with Mammy and Daddy Wynn.

Emma Jeanne was the youngest in the family. She is just four years younger than I, so while she was the "baby" I got the label of "baby brother." Jeanne is still living (2009) with her adult daughter Donna on the West Bank in New Orleans, almost out of reach of the recent Hurricane Katrina (2005). Her retired ex-Navy Commander husband (Donald Ray Thompson) died of a massive heart attack in March of 2008. [2]

Next up the scale was my red-headed sister Wilma Evelyn, two

---

[2] He was found sprawled in the floor when his family returned from Saturday shopping. When 9-1-1 was called there was a recording which said to call back Monday during office hours!

years older than I. (Many times people who did not know our family would take us for twins-- beautiful auburn hair, freckles and just about the same size!) After high school she went to work in New York, married a Swedish lithographer (Norman Salstrom) and raised a family of three: Kenny and Cliff, the sons--and Linda, the daughter. Known as Billye (her own uniquely chosen spelling!), she died in the late 1990's of Parkinson's Disease.

Two years older than Billye, we

had a sister named Nancy Jane who lived only until she was six years old, dying during an epidemic of diphtheria in the late 1920's. My very earliest memory is having my brother Ripp (AKA Charles Clifford) hold me up so that I could look into her coffin to see her one last time.

My "country brother" was Frederick Anthony and he was about two years older than Nancy. Fred married Gloria Jean King and they had two children, David and Connie.

Charles Clifford--whom my paternal grandmother (known as Grandma Downs) and _no one else_ always called Clifford--was next in line: would you believe it? about two years older than Fred. He was the first of my siblings to marry--while he and Bernice (nee Bates) were still in high school! They soon had twin boys who were stillborn or died soon after birth. Later Peggy and Butch and Larry joined that clan. Bernice and Ripp were married more than fifty years before she died, followed in a few years by Ripp.

My oldest brother was John Woolard. You've got it: he was two years older than Charles Clifford whom Grandma Downs always called Clifford but whom the rest of the world would forever call "Ripp." Why? I do not know! John was also married "early"--soon after high school--to Faye Weir whose father was a (Jackson, Mississippi) building contractor for whom John worked. John and Faye had no children and were divorced after only a few years of marriage. Since John was physically unfit for war service when World War II came along, he went into the electronics or the aero-space business, working at first for the Sperry Rand Corporation on Long Island in New York. He married a very distinctly Irish-American Catholic lady by the name of Helen Colahan and they soon adopted a son--from Ireland. It wasn't long until Helen became a Baptist and pregnant and son John was joined by two natural-borns: Cindy Lou and Virginia Ann. I am not sure when but the family moved to Florida when John's work migrated to Cape Canavaral (or Cape Kennedy--whatever the name was at that time). In 1959 Marie and the kids and I were lying around their swimming pool in Florida and John told us to "Look right up there! In exactly six minutes you will see the first ever paddlewheel satellite head for space" and sure enough, he was right. We saw it--the result of the project he had been heading up for several months.

. . . . .

So the whole family went to Sunday School and we "stayed for church" at the Brandon Baptist Church--at least from the time I was born in 1928 until Mama and Daddy and the younger half of the family moved away from Brandon about 1937, when I was nine years old. Until it was destroyed by fire in 1996 or so, I had a two-year "perfect attendance" certificate for the Cradle Roll Department at the Brandon Baptist Church.

In Search of a Unicorn

As I remember it, Daddy Wynn and Mammy were also "at church" almost every Sunday. To me, Daddy Wynn was always old--grey hair, grey mustache, wrinkled hands and face--as far back as I can remember. Some Sundays it was not unusual to hear my grandfather leading in prayer at the morning worship hour. He even taught the adult men's class, if I remember correctly. I know that he was a man whose very appearance commanded respect even before one got to know him personally. His expertise as a grafter of pecan trees and fruit trees (multiple varieties of apples and pears growing on the same tree!) and his success in raising the most tasty sweet potatoes for market and his special, secret recipe with certain herbs and spices (long before there was a Colonel Sanders or a Jimmy Dean!) that made his homemade pork sausage a bestseller--all of these were things that made my grandfather a memorable man.

He must have also been quite

remember-able for the way he drove, because I remember watching my silly brothers. They were so much older than I that they seemed to me like uncles! They would imitate Daddy Wynn's shifting his gears and then adjusting his mirror and then re-setting his hat on his head and then back to adjusting his mirror and then back to the gear shift and then the hat, etc. etc. ad nauseam. They seemed to think it was quite funny. I guess I wasn't old enough for that bit about driving to have much of an impact on me, though I do remember how special I thought I was a few years later when I sometimes went to the city (Jackson) with Daddy Wynn. He had a regular route that seemed to me to cover the whole city where he would go door-to-door to his expectant customers--always happy to see him--selling them produce from his garden, meats from his smokehouse, and in season, syrup from his sugar cane mill. It was an every Thursday trip in his long, black

1929 Chrysler.

The driving wasn't important to me, but something happened on the fifth Sunday of almost every quarter that was rather strange and to me it made Daddy Wynn especially remember-able! And it had something to do with that elusive, but ubiquitous unicorn!

Chapter Two

THE QUARTERLY SUPPER

On the fifth Sunday of almost every quarter (every three months, that is) that congregation "observed the Lord's Supper". Most people referred to it as "taking communion"--but that was really against the rules! Or so many Baptist preachers said. That word "communion" was not a Biblical word, so one wasn't "officially" allowed to refer to "the Lord's Supper" as "communion". I suppose that those preachers had never read this little portion of Scripture:

> *"The cup of blessing which we bless, is it not the communion of the blood of Christ? The bread which we break, is it not the communion of the body of Christ?"*   (I Corinthians 10:16, KJV)

No matter how strange any of the

above may seem, none of these things constitutes the strange thing that I referred to as having happened every fifth Sunday. Here it comes: My grandfather **NEVER** took communion! I could not figure out why, since he seemed to me to be as good a man as any there. What would there be about him and his life that I did not know about that would cause him not to take communion?

Well, I figured it out. He did not take communion because the deacons **NEVER** passed the plate of unleavened bread nor the tray of grape juice to him! Consequently, my grandfather never "took communion" (which was how everybody referred to what happened though, as I said, communion was "not a Biblical word and was not supposed to be used to refer to the Lord's Supper!")

Imagine!

The teacher of the men's Bible class (who often led in beautifully worded, appropriate to the occasion, sonorous, throne-approaching prayers) did not take communion--that is, he did not participate in the Lord's Supper (which "supper", by the way, was **always** held in the morning!) So I asked my mama why her daddy didn't take communion. And, would you believe it, I was told quite seriously that *he didn't take communion* **because he was a Christian!**

You see, my grandfather was a member of the First Christian Church in the capital city of Jackson, about fifteen or twenty miles away. In those days fifteen or twenty miles was a lot farther than it is these days, so it just wasn't very convenient to drive that old Whippet[3] an additional fifteen or twenty miles over not so good roads when he had already driven in from the country some six or eight miles over even worse than not-so-good roads! (Just recently, in 1994, I drove that same stretch of road, though not the same highway of course, in a matter of

---

[3] I know I said Chrysler, but that was for trips to Jackson. He had a Whippet as an "everyday" car. Remember them?

minutes!)

Daddy Wynn, therefore, usually worshipped closer to his home with a congregation of believers. Though they did not believe exactly as he did, they *were* believers and they welcomed him. To a considerable degree they had at least some of the same ideas about the Scriptures that he had. Both groups physically baptized in a *proper* way: that is, they both baptized by immersion, plunging the baptizee all the way under the water and up and out again. Mind you, I was to learn later that the "Campbellites" (for that is how the Baptists referred to the people from the Christian Church) baptized "for the remission of sins" and the Baptists baptized as a sort of "entrance ceremony" (purely symbolic) into the church (the Baptist church, that is....and make that the *local* Baptist church!)

Later I also learned that the **_for_** in the phrase "*for* the remission of sins" (Acts 2:38, KJV) is a translation of the Greek word _eis_ which in various other verses is translated as one of the following: *unto, against, into, until, end, make, till, toward, concerning, throughout, among, before, and/or insomuch !* [Appendix O]

Both groups insisted that the local congregation was completely autonomous: there was to be absolutely no control of local matters by *any* outside person or group or governing body.

<u>au•ton•o•mous</u> (-m€s) *adj. . a) having self-government b) functioning independently without control by others . . . Etymology [Gr autonomos, independent < autos, self + nomos, law:]*

I hasten to point out that in years to come allegiance by Baptists to county or district or other local associations or to state or area convention leadership became tantamount to outside control. And, without a doubt (as will be discussed later) some congregations of the group commonly known as the Christian Church (Disciples of Christ) certainly relinquished local control.

While Baptist churches (for the most part) use their own discretion as to how often communion (the

Lord's Supper, the Eucharist--call it what you will!) is observed or celebrated, I believe it is completely safe to say that among all of those congregations that call themselves by the name "church of Christ,", Christian church or even Christian Church (with a capital "C"), or the Christian Church (Disciples of Christ), the Lord's Supper is an every Sunday affair.

> *7 On Sunday we gathered for a Communion service, with Paul preaching. And since he was leaving the next day, he talked until midnight!* (The Living Bible Acts 20:5)

> *7 And upon the first day of the week, when*

the disciples came together to break bread, Paul preached unto them, (King James Version Acts 20:5)

When I was in the U. S. Army, serving as an assistant to a chaplain who in civilian life was a preacher for the churches of Christ, it was our custom to have (as Army regulations allowed) a specific "Church of Christ" worship service as well as the required General Protestant Worship Service. One of my duties was to prepare the chapel for the change of services: "Church of Christ" Worship at ten o'clock and the General Protestant Service at eleven o'clock. I had the additional pleasant duty of choosing and leading the hymns that were used in the Church of Christ worship. That was a duty that I shared with another chaplain's assistant at the General Service. He (a Lutheran) was really an accomplished organist and played the organ for the General Protestant Service while I led the singing. We shared the selection of hymns to be used--though often his chaplain had his own ideas as to what we should sing.

Since there was always communion at the "Church of Christ" worship, it was my job to get the plates of wafers and the trays with the individual tiny cups of grape juice ready ahead of time--usually on Saturday night. I did not have the problem that Catholic assistants had: they had to accurately judge how much wine to have available because once the priest had "consecrated" the wafers and wine--making them (according to Catholic belief) to become the *actual* body and blood of Christ--neither wafers nor wine could be thrown out. It was required that they be consumed. There is a well-known story in ecclesiastical history of the arguments of the monks: what if by accident a wafer were to be eaten by a rodent--and the monasteries were known to harbour many of them--would it be necessary for the monks to chase and catch and eat the rodent? We had one chaplain on the base who was quite well known for *always* telling his assistant to have on hand too much wine-- thus the chaplain had to consume the excess! (And believe me: that is a true story.)

A new, young Catholic chaplain was assigned to our

chapel and I got to know him quite well. He was about my size or a little smaller, so he was a good partner for practicing the exercises in a book that was required reading for those of us who served in the chaplain's section of the services: *Unarmed Conflict for the American Soldier.* He was not so big that I would get whomped! Whenever we were on field manoeuvres we took advantage of that off-base opportunity to learn the new techniques designed to save our lives if ever push came to shove! Because he was new to the services, to the chaplaincy, and to our chapel and to our base, he relied heavily on me to steer him in some of the things he needed to be aware of. And, reciprocally, he straightened me out on a few of the things about Catholicism that I had not learned when (as a teen-ager) I took a Knights of Columbus correspondence course to get to know what my Catholic friends at school probably believed and thought.

His help was useful in solving a mystery that turned up Sunday after Sunday. I found when I was cleaning up from the Church of Christ worship service that there were often dimes or sometimes even quarters in the bottoms of the trays. I mean, down under the little individual cups that sat in slots in the trays. Sometimes there would be as many as several dollars' worth of small coins! Why? Why in such a location?

My new friend, Chaplain Paznonskas from Latvia by way of Pennsylvania, told me his idea: some of the soldiers who had not allowed enough time between their Saturday night boozing and their Sunday morning attempt at repentance by going to church (and it did not matter to them where the church was nor what the church was) were no doubt Catholics and not being familiar with the way we (non-Catholics) did things they felt obligated to pay their dues when they took communion at the Church of Christ service: they put their contribution (**dimes** and pennies and sometimes quarters) in the most obvious place they came across: the little slots where the cups had sat. Nothing unicornish here!

Chapter Three

Close (-d) Communion

As is the custom in many Baptist groups, communion (oops! sorry! the Lord's Supper) was a closed affair. In fact, many of those very preachers who suggested it improper to refer to the supper as "communion" often said that their church practised "close (or closed) communion" meaning that non-Baptists were not welcomed at the Lord's table, at least not when Baptists were conducting the ceremony in a Baptist church building. It seems to me to be the same kind of situation that occurred in the 1796 controversy between the Presbyterians and the Anti-Burgher Seceders at Cannamaugh on the Allegheny River near Pittsburgh, Pennsylvania, when the Presbyterians were said to "have fenced the Communion table". ⁴

The strength of the Baptists' teaching about "close communion" has manifested itself in very recent years. In the early 1990's we had Baptist guests who accompanied us to worship with a church of Christ. I specifically recall a situation in which the presider deliberately (knowing of our guests) made it clear that anyone who desired to participate was

---

⁴ As reported in Leroy Garrett's book, *The Stone-Campbell Movement*.

welcome to do so: it is the Lord's table. And the ingrained Baptist teaching held sway: without exception: our guests refrained from partaking.

My questions about Daddy Wynn's not taking communion led me to some other discoveries that meant very little to me in those tender years. But, a few years ago (a half century later) I began to delve into the history of churches and religious movements, and I now cherish some of the things I remember from a-way back then.

From a different perspective, those mysterious meaningless memories from nostalgia have now taken on meanings that I could never have dreamed of then. If perchance I had dreamed of some of them, even the dreams back then would have been totally devoid of meaning!

My attendance at the Baptist church (where my grandfather never took communion) took place during the years from about 1928 until mid-1937 when my father got a better job and we moved away. He began working for the state of Mississippi as a game warden, a job that offered more security in those depression years than being the small town blacksmith with a lot of accounts receivable that would no doubt eventually have to be written off as totally uncollectible. The new job also entailed looking after a combination game reserve and Boy Scout camp near Clinton. My father had long been active as a volunteer leader in the Boy Scout movement, so the fact that the reserve was also used for summer group in-residence camping was a serendipity for the Boy Scouts. At various times prior to this our family had spent part of some summers at the camp while Daddy was there as camp director or in charge of nature studies or crafts or some such thing. In fact, I am told that I went to camp there when I was only five months old, but I do not remember that.

The new job required that our family move some twenty or thirty miles away. Consequently I did not see as much of my grandfather as I had previously, but I still remember that I respected him in every way. I cherished the visits that I sometimes made for a few days or even a week or two in the summer. True, those visits entailed watermelons and pecans and sugar cane juice during syrup making time and other treats dear to a young boy's stomach, but I also enjoyed just being with the old folks--though from today's perspective, they do not seem to have been so very old!

In Search of a Unicorn

I used to trail along beside Daddy Wynn as he did various chores around the farm always wondering what strange and delicious goodies he was going to take from the pocket of his overalls next: some new nut he was trying to grow, raw sweet potato, carrots, apples, scuppernongs[5] or chunks of sugar cane. It seemed to me he was always eating something raw and obviously very healthy as I am told by today's nutritionists! That does not hold true for one item: he

---

[5] A golden-green grape common to the southern United States

once tried to eat a seed he called a nut from some experimental trees he was growing: tung oil (tun ol)

> *a fast-drying oil derived from the seeds of the tung tree, used in place of linseed oil in paints, varnishes, etc. for a more water-resistant finish*

It did not taste very good!

Mama used to tell me that my great-great-grandfather was "a Christian church preacher." I accepted that at face value, never doubting for a moment that she was referring to the Christian Church (Disciples of Christ), which was the "denominational affiliation" of the First Christian Church in Jackson, the church where Daddy Wynn was a member. My grandfather was fifty-eight years older than I. His father (William Wynn, 1830 - 1890) was forty years older than he, and my great-great-grandfather (Watkin Wynn, 1790 - 1846) was forty years older than my great-grandfather: well, now! that poses a problem! A Christian church preacher?

[My recent research shows that my

mother should have said that my great-grandfather, rather than my great-great-grandfather was "a Christian church preacher". But the following paragraphs still apply!]

The Christian Church (Disciples of Christ) as an entity didn't exist when my great-great-grandfather or my great-grandfather would have been a-preaching! It was not until 1906 that such a designation was made, when the United States census began to list those churches that did not use musical instruments in worship as "churches of Christ" and those that did use instruments as Christian churches. That's what the history books say. But just what did those folks call themselves, back then?

The Wynn family was "East Coast". North Carolina had been Daddy Wynn's home and occasionally one of his siblings would visit Mississippi from there. In the late 1980's I happened upon a booklet that had been produced by the Macedonia Christian Church in Williamston, North

Carolina, on one of its anniversaries that showed that my great-grandfather William Wynn had on March 6, 1868, witnessed the signature of my great great grandfather Kenneth Woolard (who became William Wynn's father-in-law) on a deed for one acre of land given to the Church of Christ, such site being the home of the Macedonia Christian Church to this day. Talk about the three horns of a dilemma! *[Appendix N]*

Chapter Four

THE SMALL "C" CHURCH

Some time in my teen years on a visit to Daddy Wynn's place I got acquainted with Aunt Mary, his sister who came from her home in Texas for an extended visit. Aunt Mary was a member not of the Christian Church but of the church (small "c") of Christ. Knowing now about the twenty or more variations that exist in the Texas "brotherhood" I suppose it would be more technically correct to say that she was a member of "a" church of Christ instead of "the" church of Christ. (Actually these days I prefer in an instance such as this to use the term "congregation". That seems to clear up some of the confusion, especially if I am talking to someone who is not conversant with the semantics involved.) *[Appendix F]*

Aunt Mary talked to me a lot about understanding the Bible and following its teachings exactly, insofar as I could discern what those teachings were. And she pointed out to me *what* some of those teachings were: no instrumental music was used in worship in churches in New Testament times so no instrumental music was to be used in worship now, baptism was then and always is to be immersion only and for the remission of sins, and the early church partook of the Lord's Supper every Lord's Day so therefore the Lord's Supper is an essential part of weekly worship today. These were the basics that she shared with me, along with the confidential opinion that Daddy Wynn was not completely obeying these teachings since he was a member of "the Christian church" instead of "the church of Christ" as she was. (The Christian Church—

In Search of a Unicorn

Disciples of Christ uses mechanical instruments in worship). And so I believe that this is the time and the place where I really began my search, in a very subtle, simple, and usually silent way: the search for a unicorn.

A SIMPLE STUDY IN PSALMS

Chapter 117 is the <u>shortest</u> chapter in the Bible.
Chapter 119 is the <u>longest</u> chapter in the Bible.
Chapter 118 is the <u>center</u> chapter in the Bible

There are <u>**594**</u> chapters *Before* Psalm 118

There are <u>**594**</u> chapters *After* Psalm 118

594+594=<u>*1188*</u>

Psalm <u>*118:8*</u> is the Bible's Central verse

Who wrote the Bible?

Chapter Five

From Sunday School To Church Member

After moving to the game reserve and Boy Scout camp known as Camp Kickapoo about 1937, my family started attending a country church about equidistant from the towns of Flora and Bolton and Pocahontas and Clinton with a leaning toward Pocahontas and Flora though we lived closer to Clinton, a college town of twelve hundred or so people about eight or ten miles from Jackson in the opposite direction from Brandon where we had formerly lived.

The road from our house to Lula Baptist Church was worse than the road from Daddy Wynn's house to Brandon Baptist Church. It traversed Lime Kiln swamp with its creek that often flooded the road for a quarter of a mile at times in the winter and early spring. (I thought the name was "lion killed" until I was in my late teens and was doing a bit of mapping with a US Geological map that showed me its true name!) And then there were the many ungravelled hills, the most notable being Shepherd's Hill, about a mile from our house, where in 1953 I pulled my little Henry J[6] over to the side of the

---

[6] A car built by the Kaiser Company that was born before its

road and asked Marie to marry me, and whose adjacent gullies later constituted probably one of the largest land-fills in the state. Such road conditions sometimes interfered with our church attendance, though we were as regular as anybody for Sunday School and morning worship, training union and evening worship.

(Training Union was similar to Sunday School with classes for all ages; but instead of strictly Bible

---

time—a four cylinder beauty that cost very little and ran well.

study the emphasis was on the duties of church members, studies about missions, the promotion of denominational propaganda and special emphases, and to some degree the development of skills in presenting reports and making little speeches--a facet of the program that I appreciated and which stood me in good stead in years to come.)

The preacher often came to our house for Sunday dinner and to spend the afternoon until time to go back to training union and the evening worship. From the beginning of our time at the Lula church until I moved away ten years later, our preachers were invariably students at Mississippi College in Clinton. Our proximity to Clinton meant that often my dad or I would have to drive into Clinton to pick up the preacher and then double back by our house to pick up Mama and the girls then drive on "to church." I say "the girls" because my three older brothers were not with us at Kickapoo—they were already on their own, two married and one living with my grandparents. Those preachers who were invariably college students were most often *young* college students, and I believe that in spring and summer we had more than our fair share of Sunday dinner visitors-- no doubt due to the fact that at the camp where we lived there was a twenty-seven acre lake, lots of boats, and a pier reaching out a hundred feet or so into some of the nicest swimming water in three counties! In retrospect I wonder why I had to drive the cows out of Mr. Labon Williams' pasture so I could be baptized in his pond instead of being baptized in the slimy, slick, wooden floored children's section of the swimming area (called "the baby pen") at Lake Kickapoo. But drive the cows out we did--Merton Jr. and I.

It was at the close of an annual summer revival the year I turned thirteen. I had thought often about some of the things I had read in the Bible and heard in Sunday School and in sermons.

And I had given even more thought to what Aunt Mary had said. I believed that Jesus would forgive my sins if I confessed them and repented of them as the preachers kept saying, but only if I followed through on all that Jesus had taught!

Acts 2:38 shouted out at me as did Mark 16:16. Oh, I know: even then I had heard that the section of Mark that contained verse sixteen was "not in the earliest manuscripts", but it was certainly in my Bible and I believed it. And even now, especially now, that I am acquainted with the works of Ivan Panin,[7] I believe it is a valid part of the gospel according to Mark.[8] I walked down the aisle and my friend Merton Jr. came, too, unbeknownst to me until quite a while later though we had talked together about everything under the sun but this! And on a sunny

---

[7] A Russian agnostic who studied the Bible in order to condemn it, but discovered a numerical "scheme" that he spent his life developing to scientifically prove that the Bible was God's unique instrument.

[8] Mark 16:16 He who hath believed, and hath been baptized, shall be saved; and he who hath not believed, shall be condemned. YLT Appendix O

Sunday afternoon he and I drove the cows out of his uncle's pond and out of the pasture and we walked out into that muddy pond and were dipped down into the water and pulled up and out again because Jesus said we should—and our sins were left behind!

From that time on I never really thought much about "being a Baptist": I was just a Christian, a member of Christ's church.

Many years later the man who was about to become my dearly beloved son-in-law said it this way when I asked him about his relationship to the Lord: I am a Christian first and then a Baptist. I am pleased that he (after his own private "search for a unicorn" though I am sure he never heard such an expression) has reached a place where he now, like me, does not add the "and then a Baptist" part, because like me, he no longer is.

I knew from my study of the Bible that the church is the body of Christ and I knew that I now was a part of that body. The definition I learned in a Baptist seminary several years later stated that "a church is a local group of baptized believers voluntarily banded together to carry on the business of furthering the kingdom of God." I was now a baptized believer and I voluntarily banded together with other baptized believers at the Lula Baptist Church to (according to the best of my knowledge and ability at *that* time) carry on the business of furthering the kingdom of God. But I knew the church was more than that definition covered. The church is the body of Christ, and all who are truly Christians, disciples of Jesus, dedicated to following His teachings and His complete leadership are "members" of His church, His body. Furthering the Kingdom of God is furthering the church. To that end at the age of eighteen I asked the Lula Baptist Church to license me to preach the Gospel. And in the late spring of 1948, I did just that for the very first time.

If a shepherd is one who cares for

sheep and a goat-herd is one who cares for goats, I guess that at that time I became a unicornherd. (Just try to pronounce that!) It was my desire to preach and to teach and get others to obey the teachings of Jesus and to become a part of His body, His church. Though Aunt Mary had told me all about what was necessary to *become* a Christian, she did not tell me what to do if there was no bona fide group of Christians to worship with, so I continued for many years to worship with the Baptists, all the time seeking what I now have come to call "my church", the one that Jesus talks about in Matthew 16:18: **"Upon this rock I will build My church."**

Chapter Six

A START at PREACHING

Not only did student-preachers from Mississippi College visit our house often because they preached at Lula and because my mama was a good cook and because we were hospitable people and because I had an older sister and because there was good swimming at Kickapoo lake, several in succession stayed at our house literally living in our home as free accommodation in return for their presence during the week when my daddy was away from home driving a truck delivering tiny little fishes from the United States' federal government fish hatcheries to county seats all over Mississippi where farmers would come in from the countryside all around and bring their buckets and Daddy would dip into the big tank of his truck and get a dipperful of little fishes which he would count out to the farmers to take home and put in their ponds so they could raise the little fishes up to be big fish to feed their families or to make sure they would get a bite when they dropped their hooks into the water!

One of those preachers was

Andrew Chandler who was from Jayess, Mississippi, a few miles north of Tylertown and about ninety miles south of Clinton. He was pastor of the Magee's Creek Baptist Church between Jayess and Tylertown. I did not know it then, but Marie Rushing who was later to become my wife lived a few miles away and learned to swim in a swimming hole in Magee's Creek. She sometimes visited Magee's Creek Baptist Church. She may have been there that night (but she would have been only thirteen years old, and since I was nearly twenty, I did not notice her!)

What night do I mean?

Andrew Chandler invited me to preach my first sermon at the church where he was pastor. In later years, with experience as a preacher, I came to realize how much that invitation really meant. I know that he surely would have preferred to carry on with his program of preaching, with some particular Bible study, with some series or the other. I know that in a sense he gave up something other than his pulpit when he offered to help a neophyte along the way to becoming a preacher! As soon as he made the offer, of course, I accepted.

In connection with the invitation to preach I finagled for another invitation. I had been to Tylertown a time or two to visit friends I had met when they had attended the Boy Scout camp where my father was the caretaker. So I hitchhiked down after classes on Friday, stayed with my friends in Tylertown, relied on them *"to get me to the church on time"* for me to preach the Sunday night sermon.

Whether they were sincerely interested in hearing me preach or just thought they would be in for a good time I guess I'll never know, but a whole carload of my teenaged friends (though in those days I don't believe anybody had ever heard the phrase "teenaged") headed out onto the country roads of Walthall County: I thought *they* knew where we were going.

About twenty minutes or so before "church time", the driver asked, "Shouldn't we have been there by now?" and one of my other friends, the one I would have called my best friend and the one with whom I was staying replied, "I don't know. I thought you knew the way." As it turned out, one guy knew the way to Magee's Creek <u>Missionary</u> Baptist Church, another knew the way to a *black* Baptist church called Magee's Creek (that was long before the days of integrated churches[9]) but it seemed nobody knew the way to the Magee's Creek Baptist Church where Andrew Chandler was the preacher. Whether it was fate or luck or the intervention of God I don't know for sure and I don't really care but we rounded a curve and there it was and we were just in time!

After a rousing song service and a more than adequate and polite

---

[9] If my life depended on it today (2008) I could not take you to an integrated *Baptist* church in Walthall County—though the church of Christ in Tylertown (the county seat of Walthall County) is at least sixty percent African-American.

introduction--he really introduced the kind and generous Christian family he stayed with during the week rather than the scholarly, well read, "wanta-be" preacher he was about to foist on his faithful and trusting congregation--the pastor "turned the service over" to me to "share what the Lord had laid on my heart." There followed one of the most agonizingly prepared discourses ever delivered before a group of unsuspecting people. For the next hour and a half or two hours or maybe three, maybe four, I preached on and on and on and on and on using as my text "Let your light so shine" and as my sermon a retranslated term paper I had prepared for Spanish class earlier in the year: *Las Luces Electricas!* When I finally finished and returned to my place on the pew by my good Methodist buddy who had furnished the family's car to get us to the church on time (but barely), he looked at his watch and smilingly said, "Way to go, buddy. I like 'em like that. Exactly fourteen and a half minutes."

Tommy Downs

During my years at Mississippi College I did not have many opportunities to preach. In order to go to college I had to work and fit in my class time and study time around my work time. For the last two years of high school and the first year and a half of college I was fortunate enough to have a job driving a school bus. I say fortunate enough, because the bus not only provided a steady income, but it also gave me transportation to school, albeit a very long and circuitous route. From my home to the school according to the route I had to follow was a round trip of 176 miles per day. I continued to live with my parents at Camp Kickapoo so the bus job was enough to provide my college expenses though I supplemented my income whenever I could by continuing to paddle the boats for fishermen (as I had done since I was big enough to hold a paddle) and doing odd jobs for the Mississippi Game and Fish Commission such as cutting kudzu hay on the highway hillsides and hauling it back to the game reserve as supplemental feed for the deer. When my father died suddenly in the summer of 1948, that bonus of living at home ceased to exist since my family did not own a home but had lived for about a dozen years in the caretaker's house at Kickapoo. My mother and my younger sister moved in with my brother Ripp and his family who lived down the road toward Clinton a few miles and I moved into Ratliff Hall, the oldest dormitory for men at Mississippi

College. My father's friend, Dr. Bethea from Jackson was a constant supplier of needed funds when I could not come up with them myself. I owe him much!

At the end of the first semester I moved out. I needed sleep and I could not sleep with the noises of dormitory life. So where was I to go?

The preacher then at Lula Baptist Church owned a trailer, the kind you live in if you do not need a bathroom and there is just you and you do not need any place to hang your clothes and you can carry your water in from somewhere and you can get along without a refrigerator and you can cook on a hot plate. It was parked across the back lane from Ratliff Hall (next to another trailer that was nice and livable that was occupied by another preacher and his wife and small son.) He offered it to me free of charge for the second semester of that year if I wanted it and could make arrangements for an electrical cord from the trailer next door which was easy to do. Good fortune smiled on me again: Ratliff Hall was built on a rather severe slope and at the back half of the building there was a full height half width basement with a suite of storage and maintenance rooms and a janitor's supply room, etc. right across the lane from my trailer and there was a toilet (just a seat and a sink!) that was left unlocked all the time! I now had all I needed (the comforts of home?) without cost and convenient to classes and within brisk walking distance of the cafe where I now had a part time job that quickly developed into a full time job.

In many ways my living conditions were as good as I had ever had except that I did not have the companionship of family but lived all alone. The house we had lived in at Camp Kickapoo had no electricity for the first five or six years we were there. There was no telephone until my daddy and some of our neighbours built a phone line. We hauled our potable water in gallon glass jugs from a spring at the camp proper (about a mile from our house next to the entrance to the camp) and caught wash water in rain barrels from the gutters and roof. During the last couple of years we had access to a "running water" system, but our bathtub was Daddy-built of bricks and plastered with mortar in a lean-to kind of bathroom added to the back of the house. This kind of upbringing made it easy for me to adjust to the kind of lifestyle I now had and was later to incur when Marie and I first moved to Saskatchewan.

Bus driving came to an end early in that school year. I had driven the oldest bus in the county for over three years, on the longest route in the county, and with the poorest (hilly and ungravelled) roads in the system. The county school board kept telling me to be patient and put up with that old Chevie and they would soon be getting a new bus: "After all, the war is now over." Well, the new bus came and when I heard about it I was overjoyed. But to no avail: it was assigned to the Clinton-Jackson route, all paved, one sixth the length of my route, collecting students from upper middle class to upper class homes (while my kids were almost all poor farm kids), and driven by the son of one of the school board members! I quit my near-perfect job.

My next job was in a restaurant (well, not exactly: a cafe maybe; more correctly a hamburger joint!) called the Snack Shop. Short order cooking wasn't bad. I went in early and cooked breakfasts and then rushed to classes and then raced back at noon to fry about a dozen dozen hamburgers to sell to college students and to high school students (because the Snack Shop was half way between the Mississippi College campus and Clinton High School) and then back to classes or labs for the afternoon and then back to the grill to work from supper time until closing time about eleven o'clock. So now I had a free place to stay, all the food I needed to eat, and therefore I was able to get my four year degree in five years!

Almost.

In 1951 most of my close friends (who were in the Marine Reserves were mobilized and went into active military service. It just wasn't the same without them around. Though I was listed as a ministerial student and therefore exempt from the draft, I went to the Selective Service Board in Jackson and asked to be reclassified 1-A. When I finished high school back in 1948 I had tried to enlist in the Army but was rejected for bad eyesight. That had been a disappointment because I had hoped to save my money in the army for college tuition afterward. But volunteering for the draft worked differently. Almost immediately I was drafted and there was no mention of bad eyesight. Of course, the Korean "conflict" was in full swing now whereas in 1948 peace was trying to get going after World War II had ended. There seemed to be more need for men now than then. In what was supposed to be my last semester of college, I went into the Army for a two year term. There certainly was not much opportunity for preaching in the army! But I found a place of service and I found a very valuable ally in my search for a unicorn.

When basic training was over and the process began for slipping soldiers in to slots, I was asked what I had done in civilian life and what I would like to do in the army. Oh, there was that time or two during basic training when the sergeant asked if there was anyone who was good at typing and I said I was and I ended up deciding if this potato were the right type to go into that pot or if that potato was the right type to go into this pot and it really did not matter what kind of typing of the potatoes I did because I had to peel both pots! But after basic training the decisions were more important and more or less permanent, as much as something can be permanent in the army and especially for a limited two year term.

On the day of decision I told the interviewing officer that I had driven a bus, that I had almost finished a bachelor of arts degree with a view to going on to seminary for a graduate degree and then into the ministry, and that I had earned my living for the last four years by cooking so therefore I would be interested in being a cook.

Army policy seems to have come to the fore at this point. If you know how to cook the civilian way, you are no good to be a cook the army way! That is the way it seemed on decision day and that is the way it seemed day after day after day as I consumed army chow. Next topic!

Going into the ministry? Almost finished a B.A., but no seminary training yet? Only bona fide ordained ministers can be chaplains and they have to be graduates of Officer Training School. "And as for being a driver: drivers are a dime a dozen and ninety per cent of the recruits ask for that kind of assignment, soldier, so since you can type we will put you in the typing pool until someone specifically needs a typist. End of interview. Dismissed."

The very next day I was called back to the interviewing officer. He had had a request for a chaplain's assistant from a Baptist chaplain and his interview with me was fresh on his mind, so off I went to the chapel to meet Chaplain (Captain) William

Tommy Downs

Stringfellow, a rather small dark haired man not quite a big as I. He turned out to be a refined and polished (hold that in your memory for a few paragraphs!) "northern" Baptist, from the American Baptist Convention, I believe. Our interview seemed to be going well (and in my favour) until we got to the matter of music. Since I was not an organist and picking out tunes on my little short near-sighted mama's old pump model-with-the-warped-reeds-and-therefore-out-of-tune organ which she used to play with her glasses on upside down so she could see the music way up on the stand with the bottom part of her bifocals did not count, I was on my way back to the drill field with the rest of the as yet unassigned soldiers.

Until the next day!

Chaplain (Captain) Leonard C. Waggonner sent word to the company headquarters for me to come directly to the chapel to see him. No side trip to the classifications and assignment office. Straight to the chapel. I did not realize it then, but this was a foreshadowing of the kind of directness about him that I came to appreciate over the next two years. At the chapel I met a big, tall, raw looking, husky man whose drawl told me without a doubt that he was from Texas. I could quickly see that he was not polished and refined but as it turned out he was very definitely a diamond in the rough.

After talking about everything under the sun except the things Chaplain Stringfellow had talked to me about, Chaplain Waggonner said, "I'm calling your company first sergeant to have you assigned here and you can start work right now with filing that pile of correspondence."

Was it foolish of me to seem to object by saying "but I can't play an organ" when I knew he was a chaplain certified by the Christian Church (Disciples of Christ) of Indianapolis, Indiana, but a graduate of Abilene Christian College (with a master's degree) who had preached for many years in churches of Christ throughout Texas and western United States including a long stint in the Mormon country of Utah and Nevada? Maybe. But he said, "You did say you are pretty good at congregational song leading, didn't you? That's all I care about." Thus began another step, a *giant* step in my search for a unicorn, with an experienced guide, to boot!

Instead of Bach and Brahms and Beethoven, this chaplain I was now assigned to was a man who appreciated the music of Stamps and Sanderson and Teddlie, music I was more familiar with and which I enjoyed singing and leading!

No doubt I am the only person on the face of the earth who was ordained as a Baptist minister after a request by a preacher for the church of Christ! It happened this way:

Soon after I started my work as a chaplain's assistant, I was assigned a task of co-ordinating some meetings that under other circumstances would have been called revival meetings or gospel meetings though I do not recall exactly what military parlance was used. I did some song leading in some of those meetings. At the chapel located in the civilian dependents' housing quarters adjacent to our base a Sunday school was operated for the children who lived there. That was one of the locations where I led singing and consequently got to know a number of the people who lived there and they got to know me. I got invited to dinner nearly every

Sunday and I was asked to go with different families to their own churches in nearby towns from time to time. After a while some of them asked my chaplain for my help in conducting their Sunday school. It became one of my regular points of service: the Sunday school and then assisting at the worship service that followed. On one occasion the chaplain who was supposed to conduct the service (including preaching) became ill and I was asked on the spur of the moment if I could take over. I had to decline because I was aware of Army regulations that precluded such action by anyone except ordained clergymen.

Since I was due to go on leave shortly thereafter, my chaplain who knew the status of my education and the way Southern Baptist churches worked wrote a letter to my home church back in Mississippi and asked if they would consider ordaining me so that my talents and my services could be better put to use in the army. They did so. After that I was still just an enlisted man and not an officer and still just a chaplain's assistant and not a chaplain, but in some ways I felt a bit better about doing some of the things I was called on to do, not that ordination bestowed any special skills and powers!

I recall one interesting service I rendered as a chaplain's assistant. One Christmas I was one of the few assistants who did not go on Christmas leave. On Christmas Eve I got a visit from an almost three hundred pound Catholic chaplain who was best known for consecrating far more wine than he would ever need for any particular mass. Once the wine was consecrated it could not be poured back into the jug but had to be consumed. And who was it that was available to consume it but the chaplain!

He came to ask if I would go with him to drive and to play the organ for midnight mass at the Catholic church in the next town, a job I was not required to do since it was off-base and I was not his assigned assistant. When I explained that I was no organist, he insisted that many times on Saturday nights he had heard me playing for many hours up in the choir loft at the back of the chapel when he was hearing confessions in his office at the front of the chapel. And he said whatever I played on those occasions would be just fine for the midnight mass. Thus it was that the civilian Catholic population of Killeen, Texas, was treated to my unique renditions of *Amazing Grace* and *Almost Persuaded* and

Just As I Am and *Living For Jesus* and *I'll Fly Away* and *Trust and Obey* and just about any other hymn or gospel song I could pick out on the organ, with the occasional *Silent Night* and *It Came Upon A Midnight Clear* and *The First Noel* thrown in for good measure. And for good measure, I gladly did the driving—mainly because I thought that under the seasonal circumstances we would both be much safer!

Such incidents as that did not contribute very much to my search for a unicorn, though my army service did provide an opportunity to "inspect the herd" for a four week period during my first year when I was assigned to The Chaplain School in Fort Slocum, New York, where I met men from a wide variety of churches and synagogues and I truly believe that each and every one of them would have said that his church or synagogue was doing and believing just what God would have him to do and believe!

This was especially true of two of

my three roommates at the school. One was a Lutheran but his claims for his church did not hold a drop of water. Another was a member of a church of Christ and his discussions with me were surely as fruitful as those that I had with Chaplain Waggonner back in Texas. The three of us spent many hours of our free time seeing the sites of New York and talking and discussing and arguing about "religion" and the various attributes of our respective home states as well as our churches. We also joined the Chaplains Chorus, thrown together by one of the instructors during each session of Chaplain School.

That chorus provided me with the unforgettable experience of singing a tenor solo on national television even though even "national" television was not much in those days! Our chorus was invited to sing on the <u>Kate Smith Hour</u>, one of the most popular of the 1950's television programs. The chosen selection was Fred Waring's arrangement of "The

Battle Hymn of the Republic" in which there is a crescendo to one of the "glory, glory, hallelujah" phrases when the tenor voices are scheduled to sing "loo" sixteen times. I goofed and sang "loo" seventeen times thus launching my career as a soloist, national television, on the Kate Smith Hour! (Hmmm, what kind of voice does a unicorn have? I wonder?)

Chapter Seven

FOUR MORE YEARS IN TEXAS

After my stint of two years in the army was up, I returned to Mississippi College for summer school to finish up the classes I had dropped when I went into the army. I now had some income from the "G.I. Bill" so that I could continue my education. I also had the constitutional right to get my job back since I had actually been drafted. But Mr. Frost, owner of the Snack Shop, had hired three girls to take my place when I went into the army two years before. It was not (as one of those girls keeps telling me to this day) that I had done so much work that it took three of them to do it, but that I had worked far more hours than they could work so it took three of them to replace the hours I had worked.

One of those girls made quite an impression on me. Mr. Frost said to me very soon after I started working again that he had not had a vacation all the time I was gone so I had to take over for two or three weeks so he could take a little trip. That meant that I was the boss in charge and for three weeks I was working alone with just one of those three girls (since two of them were not going to summer school). That girl was Marie Rushing of Tylertown, Mississippi. Working closely together for two weeks we got to know each other quite well and by the end of a couple of weeks we were engaged. At the end of summer school I was off to Fort Worth, Texas, to Southwestern Baptist Theological Seminary and she stayed behind to finish up her degree at Mississippi College.

After enrolling in seminary I went looking for work and found it. At a restaurant across the street (appropriately called Seminary Cafe) I was employed with a schedule that allowed a full load of classes and I could eat free! And there was a serendipity!

One lady who worked at the restaurant (and this was a real restaurant, not just a "snack shop") was the wife of a student at the seminary and he preached at a church about one hundred ten miles away toward the east. Within a very few weeks of the start of the semester he began to have back problems and just could not tolerate the strenuous stint of driving to the church field every week, so he asked me if I wanted to take his place. I said, "Sure, I'll give it a try" and I went down on Sunday morning, found the abandoned school house where he preached and waited for the people to come. When they came (about fourteen or fifteen of them) I told them I was their new preacher. They said "okay" and so with no more complications than that I became the preacher at the

Arcadia Baptist Mission sort of kitty-cornered out between Mabank and Kemp, Texas,. I remained on that job until Marie and I moved to Saskatchewan in 1957. And I must say that the unicorn hunt was on all the while I was there.

My salary (of twenty dollars a month) was paid by the Kaufman (County) Baptist Association and another stipend (though they didn't call it that) of ten dollars was provided by the First Baptist Church of Kemp. They were the official sponsors of the mission, though I rarely saw anything of anyone except for John Stair, the preacher at the Kemp church. He and I became good friends and often shared the long ride to Fort Worth on early Tuesday mornings.

The congregation at Arcadia consisted of six or seven bona fide members of the First Baptist Church of Kemp, Texas, and a couple who were members of the First Baptist Church in Mabank, Texas. The Sunday School was run by a member of a pentecostal church (Assembly of God, I believe) and his wife. There were a couple of Methodists and a handful, maybe a dozen, members of "the church of Christ", though they did not have any connections to any particular congregation, except this!

I had about nine or ten months of baching between my first trip to Arcadia and the arrival of my bride in August of the next summer. And I made good use of that time!

The old abandoned school house

where we held services had plenty of room. The large room that served as an auditorium had been made from taking a wall out between two classrooms. That constituted a little more than one half of the space. I used old blackboards that were plentiful to construct dividers in another big classroom to create a rather snug apartment with living room, bedroom, and study. There was already a small kitchen with its own outside entrance. By the time Marie arrived in August, the renovations were complete and painted, down to the blue and pink nursery just inside the front entrance, a nursery that no mother ever left her infant in! The walls of the apartment did not go all the way to the ceiling. It was cooler that way. And there just did not seem to be any need to do all that much building when seven and a half foot walls seemed quite adequate. I guess that would have been all right except for one incident. When I came home at night I would find that Marie always waited up for me. While she was getting me some coffee or a snack, I would go into the living room, take off my jacket, and pitch it over the wall on to my bed. But one day she moved the furniture around! When I pitched my jacket over the wall it knocked a lamp off the dresser which was now where the bed was supposed to be. So naturally, being a practical man, I nailed all the furniture to the floor before I went away again.

At Arcadia we had vacation Bible

school each summer and we had a revival meeting that did not do a whole lot of reviving, but it got some people "coming to church" for a while. I did baptize a couple of people, maybe four, in the baptistry at the Kemp church building. We often had "dinner on the ground" or some such social event that made for good community spirit. I remember especially a Sweethearts Banquet that my new wife organized for Valentine's Day. It was a rollicking success with all the folks.

And then the "Campbellites" came!

They asked to use "our" building for a gospel meeting. Of course, we said they could. After all it was not *our* building at all. It was a community center that the people of the community allowed us the use of. And ironically, at that time there were more members of the churches of Christ attending our services than all the others put together. So, the preacher from the Church of Christ (sorry: I don't know if they used a capital or a lower case "c") in Mabank and some visiting speaker held meetings for a week. At first they moved the piano to the back of the room and covered it with a sheet, but then someone suggested that there was still an evil essence in the room so they moved the seats outside and the meeting continued there.

I attended most of the meetings, though I was not specifically invited. I truly wanted to hear what they had to say. I tried to be hospitable and I tried to engage the preachers in conversation from time to time, but to little avail. Basically, I was ignored!

Except when it came to subject matter! I was not mentioned by name but again and again I was referred to and not by terms that I consider complimentary! From time to time I heard some of <u>our</u> folks (who regularly attended our services but were "Cambellites") arguing with the preachers, saying that what they were saying did not apply to me! Boy, did we all have a lot to learn! But each year, after the meetings were over, the seats went back inside and the squeaky old piano was uncovered and we Arcadia folk all went on with our lives as friendly and cooperative as ever. (Since there was no one in our group who could play the piano, it sat virtually silent except during Vacation Bible School.)

After the first year of preaching at Arcadia I became known to people in another community about fifteen or twenty miles away. There the Wise Baptist Church met in the old Wise schoolhouse with a congregation of about a dozen people. They asked me to come and be their "pastor", too. So for the next three years, I would preach at Arcadia and then they would start Sunday School as I drove away going to Wise where Sunday School would just be finishing when I got there. Again in the evenings, I would preach both places except that sometimes the two groups would meet together.

The Wise congregation was a "proper" church with two deacons. The group that met each Sunday was made up of only two or three Baptist families, however. There was one family of Lutherans and about a dozen members of the church of Christ who attended quite regularly and were counted among the congregation of the Wise Baptist Church. I was preaching in two churches in two different associations and two different counties at the same time. I even received a second salary: ten more dollars a month but only if that much came into the collection plate.

Tommy Downs

Would you believe that half way between Arcadia and Wise, there was another Baptist church and a Methodist church! In the village of Prairieville the two churches and a store constituted the whole "town" except for seven or eight residences. Their school had closed so long ago that the building did not even exist. This Baptist church was of a different variety. I think they called themselves Missionary Baptists, but I am not sure. I did visit there sometimes for special services, especially "singings" in which the Methodists participated, too. And one time though I do not remember what the occasion was, I preached for them.

Working in Texas during these four years was a challenge. I had to learn how to be a husband and a father, how to preach, how to deal with deaths, how to counsel kids and parents with problems, and even how to baptize.

I think I have already mentioned baptizing in the baptistry in the church building in Kemp. That itself was a challenge because the first baptizee was a lady who was extremely hefty, over two hundred pounds. At that time I was skinny as a rail and I must have weighed about one hundred and fifteen or so!

The baptism I remember most happened at Wise. As my third and supposedly final year in seminary approached, I was in a head-on car crash and severely injured. For my final year of service in these two churches and my last semester in seminary, I was in a cast from the tips of my toes to as high up as a cast could reach on my right leg. I remember that there was some discussion of getting someone else to baptize Jerry Don and Ronnie, but I said I could do it and both of them wanted me to be the one who baptized them, though I tried to insist that the baptizer was not important—just the baptizee! My leg and its cast were wrapped in a plastic bag from the dry cleaners and taped tight. The two teenagers lifted me up and *carried* me into the cow pond (called a tank in Texas) where I stuck my crutches firmly into the muddy bottom. With big hefty Ronnie helping while I baptized Jerry Don and little scrawny Jerry Don trying to help while I baptized Ronnie, the event was completed without mishap and it even proved easier physically than the previous baptism inside of a building! And there were some at Wise who insisted that baptizing inside of a building would not have been scriptural, anyway.

During this same time I had occasion to meet the two most well-known and popular evangelists of that day--and I do not think that anyone would argue with that statement! I was taking a class in evangelism and some of the techniques of evangelism when Billy Graham visited the seminary campus. Our evangelism teacher who was always "on the ball" invited him to visit our class, where he took a personal interest in each student, talking with us and asking about our work, etc. for the whole of two class sessions.

For a class in homiletics, each of us had to write an extensive term paper on some effective evangelist of any era, dealing with three phases of his life and activities: the man, the message, and the methods. I suppose it may have been because of my physical condition that I chose to research and write about Oral Roberts and immediately wrote to his Tulsa headquarters for some background information.

Imagine my surprise when I was

called to the dean's office a few days later and asked, "What's this about a class going to San Antonio to hear Oral Roberts preach?"

I assured the dean I had no idea what he was talking about. So he told me: it seems that my request for information had been forwarded to Mr. Roberts' first class hifalutin public relations firm in New York City who in turn had phoned the dean and attempted to arrange for my entire class to be flown to San Antonio, put up in a hotel, assigned special seats at the crusade, etc., all expenses paid!

That was not what I had had in mind! I told the dean I would have no part in that because my whole report would be wrecked if everyone in the class knew as much about the subject of my research as I knew. So he phoned the folks back and suggested that I be the only one given the VIP treatment! It was agreed that my wife and daughter and I would go to San Antonio at Mr. Roberts' expense and be the guests of Oral Roberts and attend his weekend crusade. And so it was. And what a facility it was! And I do not mean the place where the crusade was taking place, I mean the snazziest motor-hotel in San Antonio, bar none! We had a two-room suite: after all a young couple could not sleep in the same room with their year-old child, could they? And we had the first hot tub I had ever seen—and not just to see, but to soak in (except I could not soak because my leg was in a cast!) And, room service! Prior to that, I had only read about such a thing as room service—but I'll tell you right now, I highly approve of it.

We were escorted to the evening services, given special reserved seats, and invited to go back stage at our leisure. (More about all those back-stage experiences later).

My first interview with Mr. Roberts was at breakfast. He was already seated when I walked into the dining room and one could almost feel a wall of ice blocks quickly arise when he saw that I was on crutches and in a cast. I tried to quickly assuage any qualms on his part by saying that the condition I was in was not a part of my plans and I did not intend to say another word about my physical situation. He relaxed and we had an interesting and open conversation about his work. To say the least, this tete-a-tete gave me a better understanding of what he deemed his mission to be and I came to appreciate him a bit more. But my encounter with him did not advance my unicorn search one whit. I did not consider his work even as a bump or a wart!

But what about back-stage?

We encountered a woman who spoke very little English. It seems she was from Norway or Denmark or some such place and was visiting her sister in Houston and they drove up to San Antonio to attend the crusades. From what we were able to discern, she did not exactly know what was going on, but her sister had assured her it was a worthwhile trip. But still she appeared to us to be quite confused about the whole situation. To be continued. (She is but one example of the kinds of things we observed.)

All right, now. The service is drawing to a close. The sermon has finished. The "healings" begin. We were startled to note that one man who was telling Mr. Roberts how he (Mr. Roberts) had healed him once before. . . Whoa! Stop the cameras. A producer or director or some such official held up his hand like a policeman stopping traffic. And the taping did not resume until that man was sent on his way and another person came up the healing line.

Eventually....

The woman from Norway or Denmark or wherever was in line. From the conversation between her and Mr. Roberts, it seemed that she suffered from arthritis (or something quite similar—arthritis seemed to be the "disease of choice") and had come all the way from Europe to attend the crusade, and of course, to get healing. It isn't easy to criticize well-meaning efforts—but something did not "set right" in our minds as we remembered our back-stage observations.

Billy Graham, Oral Roberts—I am sure I learned some important things from my brief association with them, but I learned a lot more from contact with Baptists and Methodists and Pentecostals and "church of Christers" who day by day and Sunday by Sunday tried to live their lives for Jesus. And they were not concerned with "theology" nor the ecclesiastical differences of the "churches" they were members of. And from my

Tommy Downs

association with these people I got a glimpse of a wide spectrum of unicorns!

Chapter Eight

ANOTHER CHRISTIAN CHURCH PREACHER

While I was in seminary one of my good friends was Harold Hatt from Vancouver, British Columbia, in Canada. He seemed to be engaged in a crusade to convince me that I should move to Canada. (He, a long time Baptist, became a professor in a "Disciples" university after leaving seminary!) Shortly after a crippling automobile accident in 1956 during what was supposed to be my last term of school I received a letter from the Baptist Union of Western Canada, from a Mr. Ward. He had tried for many years but in vain to get some Southwestern graduate to emigrate to Canada. After several letters back and forth he submitted my name to two congregations as a possible preacher: Quill Lake in Saskatchewan and Pincher Creek in Alberta. The Quill Lake church immediately issued an invitation to me to come to Canada and be their preacher, knowing absolutely nothing about me except the that Mr. Ward recommended me! I accepted: and for the next nine months we corresponded regularly with various people in the congregation to the point that I really seemed to get to know the place and the people long before we moved there.

I subscribed to the local papers and ordered catalogues from Eatons and MacLeods, popular Canadian retail firms. All that preliminary preparation did not really do a whole lot of good. To prove that point, when we arrived the last day of May we learned that we would be cooking on a wood stove and heating the house with an oil heater. But, there was neither oil nor wood to be found anywhere. A cistern in the cellar provided water, with a pump at the sink with which to get to it or rather to get it to us. The first day Marie washed dishes in the sink and pulled the stopper out of the drain the dish water flooded the kitchen floor! Nobody had bothered to tell us that we had to put a pail in the cupboard under the eight inch piece of pipe that served as the drain!

Quill Lake was a village of less than three hundred people with a

United Church, a Catholic church, and a "Baptist" church. Out in the countryside close by was a non-denominational, "pentecostalish" church, (after half a century in Canada, I now suspect that this was what is called a "gospel chapel", an autonomous evangelical group) and a Seventh-Day Adventist church. There were seventeen members on the Baptist church roll, two of whom were Presbyterians (explanation later) and at least a half dozen of whom I never met in all the time I was there.

In the village there was a hospital with a doctor who was shared with another village a few miles away, a pharmacy, a hardware store, a hotel with a ubiquitous bar, a pool hall and barber shop (do they always go together?), a meat market with a slaughterhouse[10] just west of town, and a "co-op". The co-operative operated a grocery up on main street and a bulk station and gasoline outlet on the highway

---

[10] We learned a new word: abbitoir

at the edge of town. *[Appendix E]*

Marie and I became good friends with Dr. Zenon Zadvorny, a Ukrainian Orthodox Church member who was dedicated to his church and to his profession. He cared for us as no other doctor ever has—and he delivered our son. He used antibiotics to keep down an infection in my leg until I achieved residency and could get hospitalization coverage for surgery because of a Texas doctor's error at the time of my auto accident. *[Appendix B]*

While I was in hospital, I met a nurse who had been the Saskatchewan roommate of my Mississippi grade eight social studies teacher when they were in college together years before!

Soon after freeze-up I received a phone call from a farmer friend (from that Pentecostalish church) asking if I would like to have a load of ice. Going along with the obvious joke, I said there was nothing I would rather have. So, sure enough, about an hour later a grain truck backed into the yard and a new dear friend, Mr. Welsh, yelled out, "Where do you want it?" All winter when we needed good soft water we simply cut off a chunk of ice with an axe and melted it in a copper boiler that was always on the stove which was always kept fired up from early October until late April.

Soon after I arrived in Quill Lake, I baptized two adults and several teens who had just been waiting for a minister to "administer the sacrament" or so it seemed! But nobody told the neophyte preacher it was also his duty to pull the plug in the bottom of the baptistry after the baptizing. Therefore, when the Christmas pageant time came around, Mary and Joseph and the angels and the shepherds had to stand on a sheet of ice to dramatize their story! [Appendix C]

From the minutes of the congregation from its beginning, I learned that the church had been organized about the turn of the century as a joint effort of Baptist and Presbyterian missionaries.

The agreement was that there would first be a Baptist minister who would serve one "term" and then a Presbyterian and then a Baptist, etc. There was to be "no doctrinal teachings in the Sunday School nor doctrinal sermons from the pulpit." *Only the Bible, mostly the New Testament, was to be used. It was to be "the Lord's church", not denominational.* By end of the second Baptist minister's term, the Presbyterians did not have anyone to send so from that day on, the joint congregation had only Baptist preachers, *or anyone else that came along and would do the job!* But a few Presbyterians remained in the town and consequently in the church: hence our acquaintance with the elderly Mrs. Bell who was still on the church roll and Mrs. Tennant, part of whose family went farther westward to Alberta and were instrumental in the founding of a Christian church in Lethbridge, Alberta and especially in the founding of Alberta Bible

College, in Calgary, where I later taught drama workshops and served on the board of trustees for several years.

After a couple of years and a half in Quill Lake and another couple of years and a half at another small town church in Saskatchewan, while not fully recovered from the automobile accident a few years earlier, I suffered severe physical problems requiring extensive emergency surgery and deep depression that required psychiatric therapy so I sought work in Regina to be near medical facilities. Details of our move to the Regina area *[Appendix M]* will be discussed later, but here I must say that during my five years on the trail with Canadian Baptists I never once got even a scent of the unicorn I was searching for, except in the adjunct groups I encountered.

Chapter Nine

Quintessentially Independent

Back when I began recovering from the serious surgery and the depression that followed it, I started working for the Co-operative Union of Saskatchewan in Regina[11] and Marie applied to teach there. Her application was duly considered and promptly rejected: she was too well-educated. Years later, under a different circumstance, they did employ her and at that time one school board official actually told me that they did not respond favourably to her original application because they could get

---

[11] *My work took me to all parts of the province, including "Indian country" in the north.* Appendix J

two teachers just out of teachers' college for the salary they would be required under the provincial teachers' contract to pay her, since she was fully qualified and properly "degree-ed". We had investigated all the small towns within driving distance of Regina and in most of them she made applications to teach.

The Milestone school had a vacancy, and as soon as they received her application and resume she was contacted by telephone and hired, sight unseen.

In Search of a Unicorn

So with my wife and two young children, I became a resident of Milestone with a seventy-seven mile round trip each day to my job in the city. We moved into rooms upstairs in the local hotel, which, as in most little Saskatchewan towns, existed more as a base station for the ubiquitous beer parlor than it did as a place for renting rooms. It was definitely not a place for a family residence. My wife made it clear on an almost daily basis that these were temporary quarters!

Tommy Downs

We set out to find a place to live. On one of our first Sunday afternoons in town, feeling "down" after another disappointing attempt to worship at the United Church, we took a walking tour looking for empty houses that looked as though they could be for sale or at least potentially rentable. There were not many, but one that had a sign saying it was for sale and that seemed suitable for our needs had about a dozen people teeming out of it at about three o'clock in the afternoon. We investigated and found that the group had just concluded their final Sunday's worship at what had been a mission project of the Yellow Grass Church of Christ. In order to get details about the building, which the church owned, we drove to Yellow Grass (about twenty-five miles away) for the evening worship. We continued making that trip on a regular basis for the next eight years. *[Appendix K]*

The "men of the church" (more about them later!) at Yellow Grass would not consider renting or selling us the house. They said it would not be a good buy and they did not want to see us stuck with a bad investment. *[Appendix G]*

We did find and buy another house, a beauty from the 1910's or so. A two-story Victorian style, with lots of gingerbread on the outside and pocket doors on the inside, it had been built by the town's druggist. Actually, it was the tallest building in town--except, of course, for the hotel where we had been living and the grain elevators. After his death his widow built a new one story bungalow next door, so she became our neighbour for the next seven or so years. That "half way house" became the site of many committee meetings and social occasions with friends from Yellow Grass and Regina Avenue congregations over the ensuing years.

The church in Yellow Grass had a preacher, it had deacons, it had elders, and it had "the men of the church." I never heard anything about a church board, or the trustees, or an official designation for the "men of the church." From time to time, an elder would announce that the men of the church would meet downstairs after the benediction, or the men of the church would meet on such and such a night. It was at those meetings that the affairs of the church would be looked after. Perhaps it was because of something Paul said:

And if they will learn anything, let them ask their husbands at home: for it is a shame for women to speak in the church. I Corinthians 14:35

Sometimes, one might be tempted

to look again and see if the men sat on one side of the assembly and the women on the other! That did not happen but it was obvious beyond a shadow of a doubt that the "men of the church" looked after the affairs of the church. There were business meetings at which all members were free to discuss matters, but even for these meetings the elders had prepared well. It was easy to see that it was the elders who exercised oversight of the congregation, but the men of the church carried out their directions.

How does your congregation deal with financing missions? Or the Bible society or an addition to the building? The congregation at Yellow Grass at its annual meeting decided on the mission projects that it would assist. Each mission was assigned a month, and all mission offerings for that month-- usually one Sunday's collection-- would go to that mission. When other requests for assistance arose, the men of the church would make recommendations to the congregation at a (usually) monthly meeting.

The Regina Avenue congregation had learned of my existence from its association with the Yellow Grass (Saskatchewan) Church of Christ, an autonomous body of Christians listed in the *Directory of the Ministry: A Yearbook of Christian Churches and Churches of Christ.* The two congregations (one "independent" and one Disciples) worked together in operating Roughbark Bible Camp for children. I served one summer as the camp's chief cook and another summer as "dean" of the "teen" camp. Friendships that proved to be long-standing grew out of those two years. I believe the fact that we lived in Milestone, just about half way between Yellow Grass and Regina, had a lot to do with the situation.

The Regina and Yellow Grass congregations were also involved with each other for decades in an organization that was called the Saskatchewan Christian Missionary Society. While I was at Yellow

Grass I was elected for a two year term as president of the society. I do not know that I can consider my election a great honour because I believe in retrospect that it was a matter of my being new and therefore one who was not likely to turn down a job that others may have considered a lost cause somewhat similar to being appointed chief security guard in charge of lifeboats on the Titanic as it left England or more likely as it neared Newfoundland! The society usually met annually, alternating between the two locations and most of the time had no membership except the two congregations! Its objective (as duly chartered under provincial legislation) was to promote evangelism and Christian education in Saskatchewan. While I was a member of the Yellow Grass congregation, I began my term as president of the missionary society. Though my presidency was coincidental to what happened, that term turned out to be the last year of the society's active existence.

In Yellow Grass, an incident occurred that adds one more to the two things I remember about the society's activities: a big black man (from Indianapolis, I believe) was preaching a powerful sermon at a Saturday night session when he pounded the pulpit and roared about the dangers of hell fire for sinners and as he pounded and pounded smoke started to swirl up from beneath the pulpit and circle around his Bible and around his hands and his head! until someone thoughtfully jerked the power cord of the public address system out of its socket!

While I was a member of the Yellow Grass congregation, I also served as its preacher. I believe that it was the very first Sunday that we attended worship at Yellow Grass that the minister announced his resignation: if it was not the first, then it was very soon thereafter. I hasten to say that my attendance had nothing to do with his resignation! He was going back to "the States" from whence he had come three or four years earlier. The elders asked me if I would preach "for a few Sundays" until they could find a permanent preacher. In those days I worked full-time in the field of adult education for the co-operative movement which was active and flourishing in Saskatchewan.

My twice on Sunday plus Wednesday night ministry at Yellow Grass continued for two and a half or three years until just about the time that I started "filling in for a few Sundays" at the church in Regina. During this time I became convinced that the Yellow Grass congregation could easily serve as the quintessential model for autonomy and independence.

About 1966 or 1967 I became the "interim minister" of a "Disciples" church. Aunt Mary probably turned over in her grave! In Regina, Saskatchewan, the minister of the Regina Avenue Christian Church (Disciples of Christ) had resigned and the elders asked me if I would "fill in a few Sundays" while they attempted to find a replacement for him. I was still "filling in" until late 1969 or early 1970! My two- or three-year interim ministry with the Regina Avenue congregation provided numerous "Christian" connections and prompted many observations that would not likely have occurred any other way and for which I am sincerely grateful. I guess there are some of those connections for which I am not necessarily grateful, but certainly I would not have had them had I not served that interim ministry.

In 1968 I was asked to attend an orientation meeting in Indianapolis, Indiana, for newly ordained or newly appointed ministers in the Christian Church (Disciples of Christ). Since I was new in serving in any capacity in that group, not even ever having been a member before, the elders considered that I should attend, and since they were footing the bill I decided "why not?" It was a convenient time of the school year, so Marie and the kids went along, though that was at my expense.

In Search of a Unicorn

The most memorable thing about that trip, I must admit, was not the conference itself, but the getting there. We flew by Air Canada to Chicago's O'Hare airport and it seemed we had lots of time to spare before continuing our flight. While wandering around the airport with the kids, by some means now unknown to me, I became aware that our flight out of Chicago to Indianapolis did not leave from O'Hare! A quickly acquired shuttle bus ride got us to Midway airport at the last moment,

Tommy Downs

and thus began the thing I remember most: we rode to Indianapolis in a plane that I did not consider capable of flying! I think it was called a Lockheed Tristar, but please, Mr. Lockheed, I could be mistaken: that was a long time ago. There was a narrow cabin with one row of narrow seats on one side of the narrow aisle and two narrow seats on the other side. I had a seat on the one seat side, right next to the doorway we went in at. I could have reached back and opened the door, I was so close to it. The plane vibrated like crazy when the engines were started, vibrated even more when we taxied down the runway, vibrated even more than that as we took off, and seemed to be about to shake apart when the pilot started getting up to cruising altitude. I do not know when I have ever been so fearful as I was at that time, on that plane. That is an experience that I shall never forget!

At the Indianapolis meeting (I think it was called a seminar) I made contact with notoriety: not deliberately, not extensively, not knowingly, but contact enough to drop it into conversations because in years to come I could look at the Disciples' yearbook for that year and I would find my name listed just one page before that of one James Jones. When I met Jim Jones at the conference, he made no impression on me at all. I do know that I met him because there were only a handful of us in that orientation group. But a few years later after he had left his People's

Temple in California and founded Jonestown, his cult colony in Guyana, I realized that I had had an encounter with notoriety. Oh, that some one of us there in that seminar could have foreseen the future and led that man down a different path!

While I was serving as the preacher of that Regina congregation I was also serving as president of the Saskatchewan Christian Missionary Society. I truly cannot remember anything that was accomplished by the society during my short term as its president nor even anything that was discussed at its meetings, with three exceptions: one was the disposal of some small property or other assets that the group no longer had need of nor plans for, another was that powerful preacher that almost set the pulpit on fire and the third was a visiting speaker by the name of Allan W. Lee, general secretary of the *World Convention of Churches of Christ.*

"This expounder of ecumenism spent one week-end in Saskatchewan. While winging his way back to New York he set down his recollections. I suggest he either has a short memory or an extremely selective one." That's what I wrote in response to Mr. Lee's post-convention report (printed in the *Canadian Disciple*) which he entitled "The Saints of Saskatchewan." I entitled my report "Bias and Bigotry."

Here is an excerpt from my response to Mr. Lee's article:

"To read about the saints of Saskatchewan a la Lee is to learn

nothing about the congregation at Yellow Grass except that Doris Johnstone is there, and Mrs. Klinck used to live there! Yet there were more Yellow Grass people at the convention Mr. Lee attended than there were members of the Regina Avenue Christian Church!"

Of the thirty-three people mentioned in Mr. Lee's article, only one was from Yellow Grass. Why? An oversight? Definitely not. When he sent me the first draft of the article within weeks of his visit here, I read it and wrote to him. I urged him not to publish it in that form. I suggested to him that it did not present a true picture of Saskatchewan's saints.

He refused to acknowledge that any editing was needed. When the article was printed in the *Canadian Disciple,* I suggested to its editor that some supplemental information about the saints of Saskatchewan would be in order. That journal also chose to print only the original article.

Mr. Lee represented ecumenism. There is no way he could be said to represent "restorationism" as I thought it was supposed to be. "Ecumenism cannot reach out unless it also reaches inward to those with common roots in the Restoration Movement," is the way I ended my report of that convention.

Leroy Garrett in *Restoration Review* wrote that the founder of the World Convention (Jesse M. Bader) complained that Disciples were so preoccupied with contact with other churches (let that read "denominations") that they neglected fellowship with each other.

He also quotes Allan Lee's claim that "the Convention makes every effort to be related to all Christian Churches, Churches of Christ and Disciples of Christ." I certainly did not find that to be true. Yellow Grass was definitely a church of Christ! Quintessential!

His lack of even acknowledging another of the "branches of the brotherhood" was especially ironic in view of the fact that the year before, the Edmonton (Alberta) convention of the All-Canada Committee of the Christian

Church (Disciples of Christ) had made two monumental decisions: (1) to talk about union with the Anglican and the United Churches, and (2) to spend as much time, money, and effort to "unite Restoration Movement" churches. It seemed clear to me that the "Disciples church" was drifting a long way from its roots, and there *I* was serving as interim minister of one of its congregations. Incidentally, it is now 2006 and to the best of my knowledge, neither of these two "monumental decisions" has borne fruit.

By the time the Regina Avenue congregation got around to calling a minister I had taken a job with the Department of Education of the Province of Saskatchewan and we had moved to Regina from Milestone, so my family and I continued to attend the Regina Avenue Christian Church (Disciples) congregation. I was asked to serve as an elder and I thought it a good thing for me to do just that. It would give me an "in" on an arrangement that I was somewhat dubious of: the congregation had called a minister of the United Church of Canada to serve on a trial basis—to see if it would work. Was I now a-drift? Well, maybe.

But not everything that happened was a drift *away*. Some things happened that were positive and some things happened that can more correctly be called neutral.

I am not certain where this situation fits: positive, neutral, or negative. Perhaps there are some incidents here that will fall into each of those slots. A project was begun to concoct a constitution for the congregation. In some ways I consider that negative because I really do not know of any scriptural pattern for such a thing. Surely though, an effort "that all things be done decently and in order" would be better than the hodgepodge that often occurs when congregations operate on a laissez-faire basis. Be that as it may, the project proceeded and was brought to fruition while I was there. One lady (Cody Harvey) especially worked long and intensely to see that a well-worded and workable document came into being.

Two parts of that constitution need mention here: There was a delineation of power and authority and ownership that favoured the local congregation in such a way that there could be no usurpation of power or authority or ownership by outsiders, and there was established a "line of action" to be followed in choosing a minister.

I mention the first item because I believe that the congregation after adopting the constitution still paid undue heed to ideas and suggestions that came from "denominatonal headquarters" and I do not mean the headquarters insisted upon by the chaplain I worked for in the U.S. Army who required me to type up his monthly report stating that the "headquarters of the church of Christ is heaven" and every month the report got bounced back to me to be revised to show that the "churches of Christ" used the same headquarters address that the Christian Church (Disciples of Christ) used because they shared with the churches of Christ in maintaining a Chaplaincy Commission for the authenticating of credentials and the consequent endorsement of chaplains. As has happened in many Baptist churches of the deep south, decisions at the grass roots almost always seem to echo what "the brass toots". *[Appendix D]*

In Search of a Unicorn

I mention the second because of what happened along about 1975 when my wife and I decided to leave the fellowship of the Regina Avenue Christian Church (Disciples of Christ). In direct violation of the new constitution, a "pulpit committee" recommended a name for a new minister to the congregation after a Sunday morning worship hour and a vote was taken right then to call the man—except the man was a woman! We moved to the Seventh and Pasqua church of

Christ, which my son called an *inorganic* church!

One positive thing that happened during the time that I was minister of the "Disciples church" concerned our daughter Melanie, then about thirteen years old. During the summer of 1969 Marie and I were both taking university classes so we allowed the children to take a bus ride to Mississippi by themselves to visit uncles and aunts and cousins and grandparents. It was quite an experience for them not only because of the bus ride but also because they were just ninety miles north of the coast when one of the mightiest hurricanes of the century tore in from the Gulf of Mexico wreaking havoc everywhere along that beautiful resort area. Hurricane Camille will always be remembered along with Katrina who came in 2005.

Melanie wrote us from Mississippi that during some revival meetings they had attended she had decided to become a Christian. But she wrote that she did not make her decision known by walking down the aisle: she didn't want "those Baptists" to think they had converted her. She would wait until she returned to Saskatchewan so her daddy could baptize her! Which I did, in the baptistery inside the building of the Regina Avenue Christian Church: she was not like the sister in the Ozarks that Carl Ketcherside wrote about who said there was no more Scripture for "one of those things" (the baptistery) *behind* the pulpit than there was for an organ *beside* the pulpit! *[Appendix L]*

This particular decision on her part led to an interesting situation in her later years when she decided to go to Mississippi College, a Baptist school in Clinton, Mississippi. The school is (or at least was) very strict in their insistence that students be involved in religious activities. A lot of pressure was put on Melanie to take part in activities at the First Baptist Church of Clinton which was just across the street from the college campus. When she was urged to become a member she said that she would willingly agree provided she could come "just as she was," (since their invitation song was often "Just As I Am".) She told them that her father was an ordained minister and that he had baptized her and that that was good enough for her so it had to be good enough for them. She thus became, I think, (as far as I can determine) the first person to become a member of a Southern Baptist church, by statement of her previous baptism in a Christian church, by a minister who had been ordained by a Southern Baptist church but who now (at that time) served a Christian Church (Disciples of Christ) congregation.

If you think that is confusing, read on!

During the time that I was an elder at Regina Avenue Christian Church and was teaching the adult Sunday School class, my wife read a classified advertisement in the Regina <u>Leader-Post</u> one night. Someone wanted telephone calls from anyone who might be interested in organizing a Southern Baptist church in Regina. I phoned the number given and told the person on the other end of the line that I was not interested in organizing a church but that I figured anyone who placed such an ad would no doubt be interested in coming to dinner for southern fried chicken, candied yams and cornbread!

He came.

He enjoyed the dinner. And though he did plead his case for

our becoming a part of his embryonic flock-to-be which soon began to meet in a school house just a few blocks from our house, after he heard us out he did not persist in his pleading. His congregation in South Carolina had given him a leave of absence to come to Regina to lay the ground work for establishing a mission or a church. He was given a few months with all his expenses paid to test the waters and do whatever explorations he thought necessary to prepare the way for a full-time man to follows. We did not establish an ecclesiastical relationship with him, but we did become friends.

A few months later I received an urgent call from Glen, which was the name of this Baptist polar pioneer whose aim was to establish a Southern Baptist church on the snow-swept prairies of Saskatchewan. His problem was that Canadian Immigration had reminded him that his visitor's visa was about to expire. The preacher he had lined up to come to take his place with the fledging congregation could not arrive until school was out in about three months! Could I please help? Thus I became an interim preacher for the first Southern Baptist church in Saskatchewan while still serving as elder and teaching a Sunday School class in a Christian church that was eight or ten blocks and five to ten minutes away! I carried on this teach-drive-preach routine for about three months, until the first full-time pastor came to serve what became

Discovery Baptist Church in Regina. And *that* pastor eventually became a Member of Parliament for his Regina constituency.

My thoughts go again to Aunt Mary's spinning in her grave! How did I get here? I got here because I wanted to preach the gospel of Jesus *whenever* and *wherever* I could find the opportunity.

Chapter Ten

MEXICO OR MISSISSIPPI?

In the sultry summer of 1987 Marie and I spent most of August in Mexico with the primary purpose of locating a retirement home. We had read a book that claimed it was possible to "live like kings in Mexico" on our Canadian teachers' retirement pensions. (I had retired two years before and Marie had only a couple of years to go.) Our on-the-spot investigations showed that such claims were only slightly exaggerated, and we decided we wanted to give it a try. We chose a spot in the state of Michoacan, a mountain "village" of about seventy-five thousand people located on the shores of a beautiful lake, about ten or twelve miles from a small village with the picturesque name of Tzin Tzan Tzun and three pyramids thousands of years old. I wanted to move to Tzin Tzan Tzun right away if for no other reason than it was beautiful and had the quaintest name I had ever heard. But it did not offer much in the way of real estate, so our choice had to be Patzcuaro.

An inquisitive and friendly and obviously wealthy motel owner (a retired geologist in his early seventies, highly educated in Spanish and in English with a wife about thirty and three preteen children (well, preteen, nothing: almost toddlers) offered us a spot of land for a song and offered to show us how to make adobe bricks so we could take our time and build ourselves a house while staying at his motel! It was almost an offer we could not refuse. We thanked Enrique and told him "muchas gracias" and came home to cogitate until Marie's time of teaching was finished. But we had serious thoughts about our new home in Mexico.

A few years earlier we had been in Mexico and worshiped with *el iglesia de cristo* and were impressed at the way fewer than a dozen Christians were carrying on a congregation without a minister in a small building they had built in the midst of their section of the city of Chihuahua. Again, in 1987 we were impressed in a different way when we worshipped with *el iglesia de cristo* in Guadalajara. As each person arrived at the building, he went to each other person and gave a big hug, so that as it turned out, every person at the worship hour hugged and got a hug from every other person! That was our favourite memory of Guadalajara.

At Christmas we took flight to Mississippi to visit friends and family. As I looked through grocery ads one weekend, I commented to Marie that food prices in Mississippi were considerably lower than prices in Canada (a fact I had actually been aware of for some thirty years but which took on added meaning after our trip to Mexico) and only slightly above those in Mexico, for the most part. She suggested that I should do some looking at the real estate supplement in the paper that weekend. After having had some surgery and still facing more, she had developed minor misgivings about Mexico—especially since she does not speak the locals' language. (I had majored in Spanish.)

Finding some interesting offerings,

we chose one to take a look at. It was about thirteen acres of mostly pine trees with a three-room house that had not been lived in (at least not by human beings) for some ten or twelve years. There was a clearing of about an acre around the house that seemed to be begging for fruit trees and flowers! The property was about ten miles south of Tylertown, and Marie's parents whom we were visiting at the time lived about ten or twelve miles north of Tylertown. We talked things over with the realtor and told her we would get back to her, and we came home to again cogitate, home this time being my father-in-law's, not ours.

Next day we started out to visit my sister whose home was in New Orleans, some ninety miles south. Since we would pass within three miles of the interesting real estate, we took a swing by for another look at the little house with the twin pines in the back yard and the big magnolia tree in the front. We still liked it. It looked like it could easily be made "home". After a half hour or so of looking things over again and dreaming, we continued on our way to New Orleans. Twin Pines (for that is what it came to be called) was only a little more than two miles north of the Louisiana state line.

The first town one encounters inside Louisiana when headed south is Franklinton. As we approached Franklinton we saw a sign that told us that the Church of Christ met at 1100 Bickham. At that moment we both spoke at once saying something like "let's buy it." It seemed that the proximity of a congregation of like-minded Christians helped us reach an important decision.

At that time we did not know of the existence of a congregation in Tylertown. We had looked in the paper and we had searched up and down the streets but we had seen no hint that there were anything but Baptists and Primitive Baptists and Missionary Baptists and United Methodists and Protestant Methodists and just plain Methodists and Pentecostals and

Catholics and Mormons and Jehovah's Witnesses and Church of God people and Church of God in Christ people and Church of God in Christ (Holiness) people living in Tylertown.

As soon as we reached my sister's house in New Orleans, we phoned the realtor and told her we wanted the house and made an appointment to meet with her.

We met with her. We made an offer. We returned to Canada. And we left it up to my father-in-law to complete arrangements and notify us of results. (This led to an interesting bit of confusion when he told Marie's siblings that he had bought a house for Marie and Tommy—not bothering to include the information that he did it with her money! One could sense an instant silent question: "Well, where's mine?")

After offers and counter-offers we became, via U. S. Mail and Canada Post and South Central Bell and SaskTEL, the absentee owners not of an adobe bungalow in Patzcuaro but an acreage and a small frame cottage near Tylertown in Walthall County, Mississippi, with our mail to come by rural route from a post office in the Pike County town of Osyka over twenty miles away--a town which we rarely ever visited!

That was February.

Marie had her surgery. She took medical leave for March and April to recuperate. In the meantime we had found and bought a twelve-year-old motor home of a design for which we had searched for fully two years. We wanted room to remodel and install a loom so finding the proper floor design had not been easy. We headed leisurely south to Mississippi by motor home, with me driving and Marie just sitting back relaxing and trying to be comfortable.

Under the doctor's orders not to lift a finger, Marie did nothing when we got there except for a superb job of suggesting and supervising and solving problems and making momentous decisions as I cleaned and scrubbed and cleaned and built shelves and cleaned and laboured away hoping to get our "new" home livable before it was time to return to Canada.

By a stroke of luck or fate or God's intervention (I do not know nor care which!) in our absence from Saskatchewan a new contract for teachers was negotiated. There was a new retirement clause that had a small "window" allowing people born at such and such a time and having a certain number of years of service, etc. to retire immediately without loss of benefits. Along with probably no more that half a dozen other Saskatchewan teachers Marie fit into that window. Without ever returning to her classrooms to pick up her nearly-thirty years' collection of notes and ditto masters and stencils and tests and other such teachers' goodies and gimmicks and my typewriter and her emergency clothing and extra shoes she retired, quietly, without even benefit of the obligatory golden handshake and retirement tea, and we stayed in Mississippi until October.

On our very first Sunday we drove to Franklinton and began our association with a congregation of the church of Christ that was different from any other with whom we had ever worshipped. A whole new breed of unicorns!

Chapter Eleven

TEACHING WITHOUT CLASSES

What we noticed first about the Franklinton congregation was that it seemed that everybody was from one family. There was the "papa and mama" and two sons and two daughters and all their families plus another daughter who lived elsewhere and sometimes visited.

Attendance was usually about fifteen to twenty, and only rarely was there anybody present except for that extended family and us and one other man who started coming the second year we were there and some times, his "Baptist-background" wife. Of course, there was the preacher whom I did not mention above.

Actually I did not mention the

preacher above, because there were the preachers—plural. One man came from a congregation about seventy-five miles north in Mississippi and preached on the second Sunday of each month and another man came from the same congregation on the fourth Sunday of each month. A local pharmacist (son-in-law of the congregation's patriarch) preached the other two Sundays and various of the other male family members took their turns with the evening and midweek activities. In a few weeks' time I was taking my turn preaching on the first Sunday morning of each month. During the "One Nation Under God" campaign of simultaneous gospel meetings organized by the Cookeville church in Tennessee, the congregation invited me to come down from Canada to preach for a week during the summer of 1995, providing our expenses, even though we had our own home to stay in.

There did not seem to be anything out of the ordinary about the worship hour. We started at ten o'clock (almost always exactly on time) and finished about a quarter after eleven. This seemed to have been a definite plan because one Sunday of each month Mr. Carruth Miller (the "papa") took everybody out to dinner, usually at the local pizza parlour, but sometimes at a big all-you-can-eat buffet that is popular in the area. Everyone was invited. Pops pick-ed up the tab. By starting our worship at ten we were finished in time to beat the Baptists to the trough! And believe me, people came to eat!

There were some obvious localized rituals or traditions and some phrases and comments that had developed in the con-gregation's liturgy, though if you asked, they would probably deny they used any liturgy! *In a prayer <u>to</u>* God—every week—one could hear these words: "We want to ***ask the Lord*** to remember all the sick and afflicted that it is our duty to pray for." Certain phrases seemed to be a necessary part of administering the Lord's Supper, for example. "We'll take up the offering at this time though we all know it is not a part of the Lord's Supper". This was stated without fail every time the plates were passed. Announcements always came right at the end when a casual observer would have thought that it was time to walk out the door. Songs were "led" by whichever man or boy was scheduled to lead on a particular Sunday. The "leading" consisted mainly of just announcing the number of the song to be sung. Singing then began with gusto.

When I took my turn leading the

singing, I *led* the singing! With my arm waving and motions to sing more silently or to give it all you've got. Some soon said that I seemed to be leading a choir rather than congregational singing. While I will admit that I tried earnestly to beat time for the music the way it was written and to vary the tempo and the volume, etc., I have to also admit it was not exactly what they wanted in the way of music. Though no one complained, I felt they would have been more satisfied with the method I once heard in a Baptist church annual meeting in Saskatchewan: Let's let them what done it last year do it again this year.

The whole family seemed to enjoy singing, and I learned that they had been well-known throughout Washington Parish[12] for their singing at fairs and school and social functions of various kinds for many years.

Without any doubt the whole congregation had been taught God's

---

[12] Louisiana has "parishes" instead of counties.

Word. Without any doubt they were trying to follow it to the best of their understanding. Without any doubt most of them were outstanding representatives and ambassadors of Christ. They were what you would call good Christians. But one thing stood out to a Canadian observer: most of the men, some of the women, and one of the preachers seemed to have to rush from the building immediately after the last "amen" to avoid nicotine withdrawal symptoms. I mention that not in condemnation of the people, but as a comment on the differences in culture between Canada and that part of the deep south. I can't think of any Christians in Canada who smoke. But, I recall something about our first Saskatchewan Christmas and some Christians and their home-brewed root beer at Christmas time!

Different kinds of unicorns must have different habits and customs according to where they are born and where they grow up!

Chapter Twelve

SIXTY-THREE SOULS in BROWNLEE

Upon our retirement, in addition to buying a little home in south Mississippi, we bought a little home in a little village on the big bare Saskatchewan prairie west of

In Search of a Unicorn

Regina some seventy-five or so miles.

Brownlee once was a thriving stop on the railway: It had a hotel, a bank, a post office, a farm implement dealer, a hardware store, a post office, a drug store, a general merchandise and grocery store, and numerous other businesses till a fire destroyed most of the town in 1928. When we first heard about its low-cost real estate it still had the farm implement dealer, a gas station and hardware store, and a combined grocery store and post office. After we moved there, the post office became a bank of outdoor lock-boxes; the gas station and hardware store burned; and the bank building was converted into a residence where nobody lives there.

We knew nobody in Brownlee: well, hardly anybody! Through her contacts with crafts people at craft shows, Marie had met a stained glass artist whose husband I had known when he was a student in the school where I taught in

Regina in the early 1970's. Just at the time we were trying to make our little house in Mississippi livable, this couple had a few troubles. He was in an automobile accident and had to have extensive physiotherapy. Since they were living in Elbow at that time this therapy required quite a drive to Saskatoon several times a week. They readily accepted our offer for them to live in our house in Regina for the summer and they transferred the therapy sessions to Regina. It was good for us to have someone in the house; and it was good for him to not have to make a long drive for therapy, only to undo it all by having a long drive back home.

Knowing then that we had retired, that we planned to spend winters in the south, and that sitting in Regina we had a five-bedroom house with all its furnishings that was now useless to us for about half the year and two thousand dollars a year property taxes, they suggested that we buy one of their houses! One of their houses?

Yes!

When they had left our place at the end of the summer, they had moved from Elbow to the village of Brownlee where they tried to purchase a certain abandoned home. At first they were unable to complete the deal, so they bought a second choice home across the street. When their first choice became available, they offered to sell us the house they were living in which had really been their second choice. So without ever having seen it, Marie bought a house in

Brownlee by telephone for the seemingly ridiculously low price of one thousand dollars. It came to be known as a "credit card" home. We later counselled some of our down-on-their-luck friends about our experience and saw them in their "credit card" homes—abandoned homes in good condition in small, almost dying towns and villages on the prairie.

We put our Regina residence up for sale, had yard sales and moving sales for several weekends, had an auction house pick up and sell some other things, and moved what was left of our thirty years' collection to our "new" house in Brownlee. We spent one night there, and returned to Mississippi for the winter!

Our friends looked after our place for us during that first winter. When we returned in the spring we discovered that Marie just could not tolerate the smell of oil in the house from the furnace so we slept in the motor home. In fact we slept in the motor home for about the first four or five years that we lived in Brownlee. The house was our house: the motor home was our bedroom.

Brownlee is approximately one hundred twenty-five kilometers from Regina. It is about sixty kilometers from Moose Jaw, the nearest city. There is a gas station in Brownlee, but the next closest town with a gasoline station is Eyebrow, thirteen kilometers away. Interesting how things like that can have a part in a hunt for a unicorn. But read on!

Chapter Thirteen

MENNONITES AND METHODISTS

One Sunday morning I realized that I had not put gasoline in the car on Saturday, and therefore we couldn't drive the seventy-five miles to Regina to worship with the church of Christ as our custom was.

There probably was not enough gas even to get us to Moose Jaw where there was a congregation of the church of Christ which we had "visited" a couple of times, but for some unknown reason we had not felt comfortable there. Even though we were retired, we seemed to feel out of place in a congregation that did not seem to have anyone younger than about thirty. I'll admit that this was a bias on our part. And I am not sure that I could document the ages of the people present, but there was a feeling, a sense, of not fitting in.

So what were we to do? There was St. Andrew's United Church a block and a half away. We had never seen any activity there—but of course we had never been in Brownlee at a usual time of worship. Also, memories of our unhappy experience trying to worship with the United Church back in Milestone meant that we did not hold out much hope of this being any better.

Knowing we had enough gasoline to make it to Eyebrow and back, we went a-looking. In Eyebrow we did see cars around the steepled United Church building right on the highway, but about half a block away there were a few cars in front of a plain front building with a sign that told us that this was the place where the Mennonites worshipped.

With some knowledge of the history of the persecutions such folk had suffered for their persistence in believing in the Bible's teachings as they un-derstood them we went in to worship with the Mennonites. We knew that Mennonites were Bible-believers, and were seeking truth, whether or not they saw *truth* the same way we did.

The speaker of the day was a teacher from a Bible college in Swift Current, Saskatchewan. He presented one of the most persuasive lectures I have ever heard on the accuracy of Scriptures and the story of Creation. I wish I had had the foresight to have a tape recorder along. I don't think I will ever hear such a good presentation ever again--and he did not have a manuscript I could borrow!

They were friendly people, but I guess not quite so hospitable as we later found the Free Methodists to be since no one invited us home to dinner! (A couple of years later, they asked me to preach for them one Sunday, and that day we *were* invited to dinner!) We were urged to come back "to church" again, and we made some tentative but unspoken plans to do so. Caught with the gas tank empty again later in the summer we drove to Eyebrow, expecting to visit the Mennonites and perhaps hear another useful and entertaining lecture. But the Mennonite church building was closed and there was no one around.

A couple of blocks to the west, on a highway corner, stood a simple white frame building with a small, short square mini-tower over its door. The sign invited one and all to come to the Free Methodist Church to worship. So we did.

The sign also indicated that the Bible was the source of all their teachings.

The senior adult Bible class was in progress in the auditorium when we entered. It was obvious that the basement was a-buzz with activity. As we learned later there were classes for all ages, and truly there were many children and young adults downstairs.

The senior adult class was taught by a short bewhiskered gentlemen who was extremely courteous toward us, inviting us to participate in the lesson discussion and seemingly overjoyed at the degree of our response. He seemed quite knowledgeable about his subject matter, and he seemed to be rather emotional at times when he was discussing such things as the need of sinners for salvation.

When the lessons were finished the crowd of children and young adults poured into the auditorium where a rousing song service ensued. There was a rather informal period of worship, with just a hint of "Methodist" liturgy showing through-

-but certainly overshadowed by a strong Biblical emphasis and evangelical fervor. The sermon was Bible-based and there followed an invitation to come to the altar for prayer or to show your decision to accept Jesus as personal Saviour. The friendly hospitality of the group manifested itself immediately after the service by our being invited by several people to come home with them for dinner. The first invitation was from our teacher of the morning and we accepted it.

Lloyd and Ruth Cornish lived in a

unique solar house just a little way west and south of Eyebrow. He was proud of the house that he had designed *and* built. It had been featured in many magazine and newspaper articles because of its unusual qualities. The thing that stood out most to me was that it had cost practically nothing to heat during the previous bitterly cold Saskatchewan winter. Marie was impressed with the big windows where Ruth grew beautiful flowers.

We spent the afternoon (until time for the evening service) with the

Cornishes. And by the time we left he had become acquainted with me and my beliefs and qualifications and training and experiences enough to ask me to come back the next Sunday and teach the Bible class! His suggestion was approved by some of the other folks he talked to at the evening service, and thus I was offered the position of being the teacher of the senior adult Bible class in Eyebrow Free Methodist Church. Before that day I had never heard of "free" Methodists! I did consult my quick reference computerized encyclopedia to see what it had to say:

> *Free Methodist Church of North America, developed from the Methodist Episcopal church; organized 1860 at Pekin, N.Y., to bring about a return to Methodism as originated by Wesley; adopted doctrine of Methodist Episcopal church with added belief in entire sanctification (freedom from inward sin) and in a stricter view regarding general judgment and future reward and punishment.*

Earlier in the day when Lloyd had first suggested my teaching, he said something like this: "Of course, we would not want you to be teaching church of Christ doctrines." I pointed out that when I taught

Bible, I was of necessity teaching "church of Christ doctrine" because that was the only doctrine in the church of Christ. He and his fellow officials accepted that, and thus I was able to accept the challenge to teach a Bible class in a Free Methodist Church, with no strings attached.

To be fair, I insert here what the same encyclopedia has to say about "Churches of Christ."

> *Churches of Christ, group of self-governing nondenominational Christian congregations; belief is based on the Bible as God's Word; religious practices are*

In Search of a Unicorn

taken only from New Testament; these include Bible reading and preaching, Communion each Sunday, baptism by immersion, and singing without accompaniment; an evan-gelistic, mission-minded church

Unicorn? There seems here to be a hint of some unicorn DNA and perhaps something will come of my working with these people—who asked me to preach only a week or two later when their preacher's father died.

Chapter Fourteen

FREE FROM WHAT?

One of my first questions about the Free Methodist Church concerned that word <u>free</u>. Free from what? There was not an immediate response to the question, though I tried it out on many people. I did not get consistent answers! I borrowed some books in an attempt to verify some of the answers I received:

Free to be totallyguided by the Holy Spirit.

Free from the domination of hierarchy.

Free to accept or reject salvation.

Free to worship without having to pay pew rent.

Free to make one's own decisions about right and wrong.

In Donald N. Bastian's book *Belonging! Adventures in Church Membership* I learned that when the Free Methodist Church was first formed at Pekin, New York, in 1860 the name came about because "the adjective 'free' reflected the issues in its origin. It was to be marked by freedom from slavery, freedom from secret societies, free seats in all churches, and the freedom of the Spirit in worship."

My research into what "free"

Methodism was all about led me into some really intriguing studies. When I shared some of the things I learned with some of the staunchest of the staunch Free Methodists, I discovered that for the most part, they were not aware of most of the theology and the history of their movement. For truly, it all started as a movement, and *a restoration movement at that!* [Appendix I]

The first news that I broke to my new-found friends concerned instrumental music in worship. Not even the oldest members of the congregation seemed to remember it, but until the Saskatchewan Conference changed the rules in the early 1950's, no musical instruments were allowed to be used in worship! Subsequent studies found that such prohibition probably stemmed from a group called the Primitive Methodists. Only a few such congregations still exist, primarily in Wisconsin, Minnesota, and Michigan.

I had studied about the *restoration* or the *reformation* of the Methodists in connection with the Stone-Campbell movement. I knew about James O'Kelly and the Republican Methodist Church. I knew of the trouble and hardships faced by Francis Asbury (a Methodist bishop) and his circuit riders in the Appalachians of Kentucky and West Virginia. These Methodist preachers like the Presbyterians and the Baptists were concerned about the worldliness of "the church" or "the churches" I suppose it would be better to say. Each in his own way was searching for an elusive thing called "unity" and most of them were finding out that it was only through a return to the teachings of the New Testament that they could find the <u>unity</u> they sought. So as I learned more and more about my newly-discovered friends who were searching for the truth of God's word in the Eyebrow (Saskatchewan) Free Methodist Church, I realized that here was, maybe not a horn, but certainly a large bump swelling up like it might become the horn of a unicorn. Later baptisms in the waters of Lake Diefenbaker by new converts in Eyebrow, gave credence to my suspicions.

Chapter Fifteen

Where the Buffalos Roam

The unicorn is a unique creature. It is grammatically incorrect to say he is the *most* unique creature one will come across because the word "unique" by its very nature declares there is none other like it.

1 one and only; single; sole [a unique specimen]   2 having no like or equal; unparalleled   3 highly unusual, extraordinary, rare, etc.: a common usage still objected to by some

At least six times the *King James (Authorized) Version of the Holy Bible* refers to the unicorn! So, in searching for a unicorn, why bother with something that is not unique? Buffalos, for example. The prairies used to be filled with them. Even now, there is a return to the roaming of the buffalos, because in their search to make a living when the wheat won't sell, the ever resourceful Saskatchewan farmers are trying new things--if buffalos can be called new!

On a recent return to Brownlee (the village of sixty-three souls-- minus two because we moved away in 2001) Marie and I saw a sign about four feet by six feet just a block from what used to be our house, a sign offering ELK MEAT FOR SALE. So what's the connection? Buffalos, unicorns?

In Search of a Unicorn

Remember my opening pages and a reference to "bumps and warts that may try to pass as horns"? And do you remember my having to point out to the Free Methodist folks--even the oldest of the old-timers—that they used to have no mechanical musical instruments in their worship, just the beautiful, melodious God-given instruments of voice? Well, in a sense and from a distance, buffalos may appear to some people to have humps!

And indeed, the waters of Lake

Diefenbaker, held in place by the world's (at-that-time) largest dirt dam became the Galilee or the Jordan for a few Scripture-studying seekers who found their unicorn while roaming with the buffalos!

About ten miles north of Brownlee was located the Huron Colony of the Hutterian Brethren. I got acquainted with them when I needed a plumber and went to the local hardware store. The owner of the store told me that there was a good plumber at the Hutterite Colony and I asked his name. I was told that because of their colony's restrictions on their members working away from the colony I could not contact him directly. "Just be patient. I'll have him call on you soon." True to the hardware man's word, in a few days I had a visit from Martin Kleinsasser--the plumber from the Hutterite Colony. He did the work I needed done, and when I asked him how much I owed him, he declined to give me a price. He did say to me that he really did like my pocket knife--which I determined was his way of saying he would settle for it! Since my pocket knife was a Swiss Army knife that my wife had bought for me when we were walking the streets of Lucerne, Switzerland, a summer or two earlier, I could not part with it. However I was able--without too much trouble—to get Martin to accept a twenty dollar bill, with a hint from him, that no one was really to know about the transaction. (So please don't tell).

A couple of years later a situation occurred which allowed me to make up somewhat for the good deed done for me. Martin stopped by to admire the huge yard full of flowers of many colours that surrounded our house and gardens (we had six lots!). He did not recognize the flowers but he thought they would be really good for their bees--especially when I told him how prolific they were and how quickly and profusely they grew. So when fall came, I collected ice cream pails[13] full of larkspur seeds for them to

---

[13] Practically a standard measure in Saskatchewan!

plant to feed the bees at the Huron Colony of the Hutterian Brethren!

Visits to the colony were a tourist attraction when we had guests. Marie's sisters were welcomed as was her father. They, of course, had never seen such a place. The huge kitchen with its gleaming stainless steel appliances and cookware fascinated the Southern ladies on their visit. The most modern of farm equipment in a similar manner fascinated my father-in-law who had been both a heavy equipment operator *and* a cotton farmer in Mississippi.

I was never fortunate enough to get invited to a meal, but Marie at least once partook of food with them, at a time when her sisters were visiting Saskatchewan from Mississippi. (The sisters were surprised to find the Hutterite girls were crazy about country singers!)

My interest was in their "church." They have a special room big enough for everyone in the colony to meet at once. It is a plain and simple facility with the seating divided down the middle, so that the men and boys can sit on one side and the women and girls on the other. There is a plain table in the centre of the room at one end where the Bible sits--a big, Holy Bible, in German. There is no musical instrument. And while I did not attend a worship service there, I was told about it: simple, singing, music by voices only, and a sermon by the preacher who is assigned the job just as the "pig boss" or the "cow boss" or the "tractor boss" or the "garden boss" is assigned his job. You take the assignment that the colony considers you best for and you do your best at that job. The sermons are all ***read from hand-written collections*** handed down since the 1600's!

In his book *The Forgotten People* Michael Holzach said something like this:

I'm not saying that the shepherd of the flock has to be a great intellectual, but certainly you look at men like Paul, or early Christians like Justin or Tertullian, and they had a command of the Scriptures and an ability, a divinely inspired way, to relate with other human beings and convict them regarding the truth of the Gospels.

Baptism seems to be routine. Along about Easter men or women in their mid-twenties are baptized and after that must give up their hidden radios and guitars and cosmetics, etc. If after that they participate in worldly ways, and refuse to repent, they are likely to be banished from colony!

Back at the Free Methodist Church one Sunday, I had a discussion--bordering on an argument--with the teacher of the other adult class. (I taught the senior adults). There was some comment by someone that you had to watch the Hutterites if they came in your home or your yard or your place of business--because they would steal. In a simple conversation with me he commented that the Hutterites in their religion taught that it was all right to steal as long as you did not get caught! I disputed that with a vehemence. I knew from previous studies that their religious beliefs were Bible-based and such a preponderant matter would not be corrupted in that way. We did not settle our "discussion" but I did not need to: I knew I was right.

When all things are considered--their history, their simple beliefs, their commonality when it comes to worship--what I learned about the Hutterites told me that there is unicorn blood somewhere there in their heritage!

Chapter Sixteen

Men of "The Word"

Along about 1967 when I began preaching for the Regina Avenue Christian Church (Disciples) in Saskatchewan's capital city of

Regina, I accidentally received something of a legacy, from Owen Still, whose father had ministered many years in Hawaii and who himself (Owen, I mean) could have been the quintessential model for Bill Gates' idea of Microsoft's system of multi-tasking because Owen was a multi-tasker *par excellence*: as the preacher, (the pastor, the minister) of the "Disciples Church", he was also the chaplain to the students of the University of Saskatchewan (Regina Campus), later to become the

In Search of a Unicorn

University of Regina and instigator of help for people shackled by alcohol in his work with Alcoholics Anonymous--who still regularly met in the basement of the church building when I was preaching there in the late sixties; and he was often pulpit supply for United Church congregations all around central Saskatchewan. The legacy I refer to was a two- or three-foot shelf of copies of booklets and pamphlets, and especially the *Mission Messenger*, a succinct and Godly periodical edited and mostly written by the (once obnoxious, fast-becoming ancient and soon to retire and then go to his heavenly reward) Sage of the Ozarks by the name of Carl Ketcherside—copies which Owen had (reluctantly, I am certain) relegated to the trash can.

In two different summers I had been blessed by sitting on a log praying with and talking to and learning from Carl, somewhat hoggishly occupying every possible minute of his after-lessons time at the widely attended (by Canadians and Americans alike) family Bible camp that was a true representation of the so-called Restoration Movement, with campers from churches of Christ, the (Independent) Christian Churches and Christian Church (Disciples) peacefully situated down deep in a tree-shaded coulee on the prairie farm of Elgin Banting who loved the Lord and could cook cracked wheat all night long so that everyone could have a nourishing breakfast <u>that would stay with you.</u> It was here that I met Carl and other outstanding Christian leaders: men like Boyd Lammiman, the president of Alberta Bible College in Calgary; his successor, Ron Fraser; Leroy Garrett, author of ***The Stone-Campbell Movement*** and editor of **Restoration Review**, which almost rivaled **Mission Messenger**; Alan Dunbar, who later had the glorious honour of announcing to all of us who were attending the Billy Graham Evangelism Seminar at Hotel Lake Louise on the night of the Quebec Referendum: "We still have a country"; a little boy who became Dr. Dwayne Banting, professor first at Maritime Christian College in Prince Edward Island and then at Briercrest Seminary in Caronport, Saskatchewan; another little boy named Leslie Williams who later served the Lord faithfully as a missionary in Papua New Guinea and Jim Williams, his father who served First Nations people as no other man has ever done; Ed Benoit, Godly Alberta politician extraordinaire; and Dwayne Dunning, who was instrumental in having me teach drama to Bible college students in Huron, South Dakota, and direct there a play I wrote which was seen by a wayward student seeking how he could serve the Lord with his interest in drama and was so inspired by the play that he consequently formed a drama group that did promising work throughout the Midwest after seeing my play, "*The Design of A Random Pattern,*" etc. Etc. Etc.

But it is Carl that stands out most

in my memory of Macrorie Camp, because of one particular thing he said: "Wherever God has a son, I have a brother!" Carl himself said that halfway through his ministry he changed: *"a peacemaker instead of a piecemaker."*

I was so impressed by Carl's writings that when College Press of Joplin, Missouri, published a multi-volume set of *The Writings of Carl Ketcherside* I bought three sets: one for the library of Alberta Bible College in Calgary; one for the library of Western Christian College then in Weyburn, Saskatchewan, now in Regina; and one for me—which I later gave to a young Christian who was born on my fifty-ninth birthday, Ben Thiessen of the Saskatchewan town of Eyebrow. So if I liked those books so much, why did I give mine away? Well, the internet came along and I found I could read any and all of Carl's writings on my computer screen—as can you—at *www.unity-in-diversity.com*. One of Carl's books is entitled *The Twisted Scriptures.* In that book he zeroed in on specific sections of The Word that through the ages have been mis-read or mis-represented. An example of this that stands out in my mind is Amos 3:3: *"Can two walk together, except they be agreed?"*

Brother Ketcherside explains that the *agreement* involved is simply an agreement to get together and walk together—not that they must agree on everything! Can two go together if they have not settled on a place to start the journey? They must agree on that—then they can walk together. For my purposes, I look at the

Tommy Downs

Scriptures that are twisted in a slightly different way.

Often in a talk to children—what some call a children's sermon—as a teaser in a talk, or just as a point of emphasis, an illustration, I will give a little quiz that asks among other things this question: "Which does the Bible say more about, cats or unicorns?" To most folks, since unicorns are mythological critters, the answer is obvious. And for cat lovers it is quite a shock to learn that their beloved pets are not even mentioned in God's Word! But unicorns are!

In Search of a Unicorn

Num 23:22 God brought them out of Egypt; he hath as it were the strength of an unicorn .

Job 39:9 Will the unicorn be willing to serve thee, or abide by thy crib?

Job 39:10 Canst thou bind the unicorn with his band in the furrow? or will he harrow the valleys after thee?

Ps 29:6 He maketh them also to skip like a calf; Lebanon and Sirion like a young unicorn .

Ps 92:10 But my horn shalt thou exalt like the horn of an unicorn : I shall be anointed with fresh oil.

Num 24:8 God brought him forth out of Egypt; he hath as it were the strength of an unicorn : he shall eat up the nations his enemies, and shall break their bones, and pierce them through with his arrows.

Ps 22:21 Save me from the lion's mouth: for thou hast heard me from the horns of the unicorns .

Isa 34:7 And the unicorns shall come down with them, and the bullocks with the bulls; and their land shall be soaked with blood, and their dust made fat with fatness.

Ps 22:21 Save me from the lion's mouth: for thou hast heard me from the horns of the unicorns .

Now it is obvious that "unicorn" in these verses does not refer to anything even remotely concerning the "church." And my use of the word in my title and in my references near the end of each chapter is just a metaphor! Why? Because of the unicorn's uniqueness—and the church's uniqueness. The church, the kingdom, the body of Christ! There is nothing like it! It is unique! There is no other Way under Heaven whereby we must be saved! The church, the kingdom, the body of Christ! It is unique! Do we have all the answers? Do you? I don't. But I am willing to keep seeking, to keep searching. As I come upon new truths—new to me, but as old as God—I must incorporate them into my beliefs, into what I teach to others. And I know that that body of beliefs will still be unique—because it is of God.

The Appendices

A	A Communion Meditation.	(Poem)	Page 345
B	Things Not Meant to Be .	(Poem)	Page 347
C	A Christmas Prayer	(Poem)	Page 350
D	My Philosophy of Education.	(Essay)	Page 358
E	Two Peas in a Pod	(Short Story)	Page 377
F	An Alphabet of Churches	(Listing)	Page 401
G	Some Men Who Tried	(Listing)	Page 411
H	The Gospel According to Gimpy	(Short Story)	Page 417
I	O'Kelly's Plan of Union	(Essay)	Page 429
J	The Promise	(Short Story)	Page 442
K	The Silver Trombone	(Short Story)	Page 461
L	The Question Mark Mind	(Poem)	Page 485
M	Butcher	(Short Story)	Page 492
N	Macedonia	(Historical)	Page 502
O	The Meanings of "EIS"	(Listing)	Page 507

A SECOND Study in Psalms

William Shakespeare

Was 46 years old when the King James
Bible was introduced to the world.

Turn to Psalm 46 in your own copy of the
King James (Authorized) Bible

Count the words
Look closely at the 46th word

Go to the end of the Psalm
Count up!

Look closely at the 46th word
From the End!

Who wrote the Bible?

APPENDIX A

A Communion Meditation

The blood spurted out when He died

And the soldier thrust in the spear

But the blood oozed out when He prayed

With His sweat - with a tear

Words spurted out in anger

When the temple was over-run

But the compassion oozed out for the men

And for the wrongs that they had done

The miracles spurted out His power

In Search of a Unicorn

They showed from whence He came

The trial oozed out the questions

Who are you? What is your name?

The glamour and popularity spurted out

And some people flocked around Him

His personality oozed out with a magnetism

While others had to search 'til they found Him

With evangelistic zeal and fervor

We sometimes spurt out against sins

But with our day by day living

We ooze out the witness that wins.

© 1968 Tommy Downs

APPENDIX B

(a poem I wrote while I was in hospital one Christmas day)

THINGS NOT MEANT TO BE

Room three-twenty-six

All sterile and white

Antiseptic-smelling

Like an OR extended.

Seven o'clock: blinds zip

Morning sun bright

Reveals myriads of multitudes nature never

In Search of a Unicorn

intended

Like a little boy in hospital on Christmas day

Six loud-mouthed visitors each having his say

    Sores on the back where long I have lain

Three-hour pain-killers for four-hour pain

Personal-use earphones turned up full blast

    Someone wrote obscenities on the foot of a cast!

Penicillin's caused someone's face to go spotty

    They ask a 97-year old man if he wants to go potty.

An un-urined urinal

Holds long-stemmed roses

    Ten o'clock night nurses

Tommy Downs
Bring night-time doses

"Wake up, Joe!

    Take your sleeping pill"

A hospital's no place for a guy when he's ill!

© 1959 Tommy Downs

APPENDIX C

A Christmas Prayer

>Our Father, who art in Heaven . . .

But who, nearly two millennia ago

According to the angel Gabriel whom You sent unto a city of Galilee named Nazareth...

Our Father, who art in heaven........

>But who, nearly two millennia ago

>Came as a Holy Spirit to that virgin

Tommy Downs

    espoused to a man whose name was Joseph of the house of David —

    And the virgin's name was Mary. . .

Our Father, who art in heaven.....

    But who, nearly two millennia

    but nine months later

    Came into Judaea, unto the city of David,

      Came into Judaea, unto the city of David

        which is called Bethlehem,

        and was brought forth as Mary's firstborn son,

and wrapped in swaddling clothes and laid in a manger;

because there was no room for You in the

inn...

Our Father, who art in heaven

> But who, nearly two millennia ago
>
> Was announced to shepherds on a hillside by a multitude of angels — the heavenly host, praising God, and saying
>
> Glory to God in the highest, and on earth peace, good will toward men...

Our Father, who art in heaven

But who, nearly two millennia ago

Attracted the attention of wise men

Who saw Your Star in the east, as it went before them,

> Till it came and stood over where You were!
>
> > causing them to rejoice with exceeding

great joy,

    for when they were come into the house,

They saw You with Mary your mother,

    and fell down, and worshipped You:

    and when they had opened their treasures,

    they presented unto You gifts;

Gold, Frankincense, and Myrrh.

Our Father, who art in heaven. . .

Same Father. . .

    Same Spirit. . .

        Same Son!

    Same Father

who created the whole universe-even the parts that man just now   thinks he is discovering.

Same Father

 who knows all there is to know about everything

even about the tiniest details of each and every one of us.

Same Father . . .

 who loves us despite of our erring ways and is ready and willing to forgive our sins.

Same Spirit . . .

who descended like a dove upon the Son as He rose from the waters of Jordon at His Baptism. . .

Same Spirit . . .

who descended like flaming tongues on the inauguration day of Your church. . .

Tommy Downs

Same Spirit . . .

who entered into each of Your children at the time he accepted Your Son as his Saviour.

Same Son:

    who increased in wisdom and stature,

    and in favour with God and man.

Same Son:

    who taught and preached the Good News...

Same Son:

    who was crucified and rose again...

Before You, O God,
              we come to praise.

Before You, O God,

In Search of a Unicorn

   we come to express our gratitude
for Your goodness to us.

Before You, O God,

  we come to plead for health and
  comfort for those who are ill,
  injured and in despair

Before You, O God,

  we come to ask

   for safety for those who travel;

   for guidance for those who are
   trying to find

  where to go and what to do;

And, O God, we beg for forgiveness

 for those things we have done

 that we should not have done and

Tommy Downs

for those times when we did not do

    what we should have done.

We pray for the grace

    to avoid unfair judgment of those with whom we differ,

We pray for the patience

    to listen to those with whom we disagree,
and   We pray for the love

    to reach out to those from whom we may be divided when we ought to be together in You!

In the name of the Baby of Bethlehem who now is the King on High!

Amen. Amen. And again, I say Amen!

APPENDIX D

My Philosophy of Education

© 1968 Tommy Downs--Published in *The Lookout* and *The John Milton Magazine for the Blind* in 1969

I am a definite, deliberate, and determined disciple of a Being born in Bethlehem two thousand years ago. There were no more than a few miles between the busy barn where He was born and the stark, stony, sun-baked crag where He was put to death about thirty-three years later. He hardly left His hometown neighbourhood . . . from Bethlehem, to Bethany, a quick trip to Egypt to save His skin, to Nazareth, from Galilee to Gethsemane. Yet, the traffic of the world passed His door: the statesmen from Rome, the doctors from Greece, the grain buyers from Egypt, the scientists from the Orient, the mariners from the Mediterranean! And He learned of life as they passed: life with its trials, its troubles, its temptations, its testings, its terrors. But He also knew friendships and family relations. He felt compassion for others. He experienced outbursts of emotion-cleansing anger. He knew and recommended the joy of abundant living.

This man I call "Master" is more than man. He is an inspiring instigator, a lucid leader, a motivator of men, the essence of enthusiasm for His cause. He was a nonconformist. He was a carpenter. He was a psychologist. He was a philosopher, and He was a master-teacher. From recorded history, I know this.

Jesus used techniques and methods that are (even today!) recognized and recommended as highly effective means of communication.

1. He used the precise language of the people to whom He talked. He talked about fishing to fishermen, about crops to farmers, sheep to shepherds, money to tax collectors. He used wry wit and

subtle humour and puns galore! His apt illustrations and pertinent parables got the message across!

2. He knew the value of audiovisuals. Ever hear the story of the little boy and his lunch? Jesus used his five loaves and two fishes to feed five thousand people. And what about that participatory creative drama in an upper room—a drama that has been re-created weekly in hundreds of thousands of places of worship around the world and in a greatly modified version every day, some place.

Even His death set up a symbol that has stood the test of time. No market research technique today has produced a corporate identity-- a logo--equal to the cross of Christ!

3. His system was involvement with a capital I. He demanded absolute commitment. His method of teaching His followers to win others to His way was simply to send them out two by two to do the job. Most teachers agree that students remember best those things in which they themselves are actively engaged.

The teachings of Jesus so permeate my whole being that my philosophy of education has to be a Christian philosophy. Now, notice that I did not say "the" Christian philosophy, I said "a" Christian philosophy! There is a. difference.

But it is a Christian philosophy: fluid, fluctuating, firmly-rounded, but flexible! This multi-faceted philosophy glows and glimmers and glistens with some inner glory, I suppose, but mainly its many faces faithfully reflect from all around, those qualities that it recognizes as worthwhile.

Here is what I mean:

Socrates said that the unexamined life is not worth living. Jesus agreed. "Let a man examine himself," He said. Not his neighbour!

Jesus said: "Judge not, that you be not judged"

It is true that the Christian concept of faith cannot very well be "proved" to someone who does not have it. But how far away from each other are these two ideas?

2   Aristotle: The unmoved mover can have no connection with matter. Jesus: God is Spirit and those who think Him worthy of reverence must pay their respect to Him in a spiritual way. Aristotle taught that the potential is meaningless without practice. Good! The Christian philosophy says that faith without good works is lifeless. Christians are admonished not only to listen to their Lord's words, but to do what He says.

3. Plato suggested tackling one problem at a time and conquering it before starting on another one. Jesus said that His disciple should first remove the log from his own eye and then he could see more clearly to remove the sliver (or toothpick) from another's eye. For Plato, life was a gradual progression from the uncertainties around—through degrees of enlightenment—to the Absolute. Paul of Tarsus—a Christian philosopher—said, "Now we see as through a dirty glass, dimly; but

later we shall see clearly, face to face."

4. Descartes had a good idea: I am thinking; therefore, I am. A similar statement by Jesus sounds more absolute, has no qualifications attached, and (with me, at least!) carries more weight: "I am that I am."

5. What shall I say of Kierkegaard? Well, I agree with much that he had to say about the established church or established Christianity. Because "Established Christianity" in his day was (as it is

in mine) a far cry from the simple "Way" proclaimed by the Christ. Kierkegaard's "knight of faith" is, I suppose, the hero I would emulate. Like Kierkegaard, I disagree with Hegel. After all, it just is not rational to turn the other cheek as suggested by Jesus. But some who've tried it will say it works!

6. Nietzsche? One budding philosophical poet wrote, "Nietzsche is pietzsche!" I cannot agree. I don't think he tried very hard to know what Jesus taught.

"Christianity considers all people equal"? Hog-wash! Jesus talked about men as the rich and the poor, the sick and the well, the master and the slave, the wise and the fools, the wheat and the chaff, the sheep and the goats. That's equality?

7. Was it Jean-Paul Sartre who came out with the profound statement that affirms "that which is, is, what it is not, and that is not what it will be." It was Paul who said: that which I would do, do I not; and that which I would not

do, I do. And he said we are now learning what we are, but we do not know what we will someday be.

So what is my philosophy of education?

Here are some statements that apply to most areas of human relations. That of course includes teaching. And teaching is a vital part of education.

1. I believe my experience in confronting the challenge of Christ and deliberately deciding to be His

disciple is real. I believe that that experience influences everything I do. I suppose, therefore, I could be called a Christian *empiricist.*

2. I believe I should treat others as I would like others to treat me in similar circumstances. Simple? Too simple? Perhaps. But I know it works. That makes me a *pragmatist.*

3. I believe "all things should be done decently and in order" (as Paul wrote). So I guess I am in a sense a *teleologist.*

4. I believe that I must accept responsibility for my deliberate actions and for the results that grow out of my deliberate actions. Does that make me a *determinist?*

5. I believe I should share the good news (of my satisfying experience as a follower of Jesus) with others who seem to me to need the experience I have had . . though all the time respecting the right of others to refrain from response.

6. I believe I must treat every individual with the dignity due

another human "soul," whether he be a student under my supervision or an administrator under whose supervision I work. I must share my knowledge and my skills and my *self* with those who can benefit from such sharing. This—in a small way—is the kind of compassion that Jesus had.

Jesus told His disciples, with clarity, what their role in society is to be: Salt. Light. Leaven. As "salt of the earth" I must play the Christian role of helping to bring out the true flavour of the society I live in. As "light of the world" I must not keep unto myself, but must share and radiate—responding to the needs around me and making the path to abundant life clear and easy to see. The lump of leaven gives life to the loaf. As leaven, I must remember that I am not the loaf. But I am a vital part of the loaf. The quality of the loaf depends on the liveliness of the leaven.

This responsibility I accept.

What I Learned From Old Brother Noah!

1. Don't miss the boat.
2. Remember we are all in the same boat.
3. Plan ahead. It wasn't raining when Noah built the ark.
4. Stay fit. When you are 500 years old someone important may ask you to do something big.
5. Don't listen to critics.
6. Build your future on high ground.
7. Always travel in pairs.
8. Speed isn't everything: the snails were there with the cheetahs.
9. When you get stressed out, just float around a bit.

ABOVE ALL, REMEMBER:

The Ark was built by an amateur. It was the Titanic that was built by the professionals.

(Copied from a whole bunch of internet items over a long period of time.)

APPENDIX E

Two Peas In A Pod

On hoar-frosty mornings in the early and mid-fifties the mail trains moved from pearl to pearl along the shimmering strings called **CP** and **CNR**. At each jeweled village along the way somebody had to meet that train and trade the out-going mail for the in-coming mail.

And somebody had to get those bulky gray bags of mail from the station to the post office and from the post office to the station. Somebody had to get up early and somebody had to stay up late...if that's the way the train's schedule happened to run. That somebody had to be dependable, and responsible, and punctual—always on time.

In our town that somebody was Tinker the Clinker—and moving Her Majesty's morning and evening mail was the only thing Tinker the

Tommy Downs

Clinker was ever known to be dependable about, responsible for, or on time—no! that's not quite true. He definitely was on time for two other things. The first thing he was always on time for was the eleven a.m. opening of the beer parlour at the local five-room "ho—el". (The "T" had dropped off the sign the week after it was put up and no one ever bothered putting it back up. After all, no one ever came around looking for a place to stay, only a place to get a beer). The other thing he was always on time for was the seven o'clock after-supper opening of the same establishment. But he never missed the mail until that day. . But more about that later. You need to know about Tinker's house,

Tinker's place was what you might call a modest home—if you were not careful with words and if you didn't really know what modest means! Tinker's home was on the right side of the tracks—and by that you are to infer "proper" side of the tracks. It wasn't like those shanties

Tommy Downs

on the south side beyond the grain elevators where all the shady-skinned foreign section hands who hardly spoke English lived. Actually it was on Second Avenue alongside the pink and purple and orange and blue and green cottages where the retired Ukrainian farmers' wives and widows who hardly spoke English lived. Two blocks east was Central Avenue with the usual array of small, small-town shops: Axel's Shoe and Harness Shop (though no one could remember, not even Axel, when he last repaired any harness and it was getting so few people had their shoes repaired anymore either!), the Red and White store—trying hard to keep its customers happy with a new co-op grocery just opening up half a block away and most of the folks in town at least semi-socialists, not federally just provincially; D'Tritre's Drugs, with rooms up over for the family that consisted of the druggist, his wife, his son, and the wife's father; Joe's Pool Room and Barber Shoppe shared quarters with Joe

Tommy Downs

Small Appliance Repairs—and Joe did odd-job carpentry and plumbing in his spare time which he had lots of. All in all it was a fairly typical small-town main street, except somebody way back somewhere had made a slight mistake and run the streets the way the avenues were supposed to run and the avenues the way the streets were supposed to run so that "main street" was Central Avenue.

Two blocks east of Tinker's house, Central Avenue; one-half block west of Tinker's house was the treeless edge of a treeless prairie that reached treeless-ly across forty or fifty treeless miles to the treeless edge of Assiniboldt City, prematurely misnamed by a railroad crew chief who never dreamed the population would never pass two thousand.

Tinker's house had a fence, broken down. Tinker's house had a garden, overgrown with weeds. Tinker's house had a porch, with most of the boards broken through. There was a screen door with no screen, a storm door with no latch and only one hinge, and then there was the inside. Wow! Only the vividest imagination could concoct such a scene as the inside. Beer bottles literally were knee-deep: not boxes of beer bottles neatly-stacked, but bottles—broken and whole—literally knee-deep. An oil space heater scorched black and coated with soot from lack of attention stood in one corner of what appeared to be the only room. All around on tables and chairs and even under some sat tin cans, seemingly smashed open with an axe or a hunting knife, some half-emptied, some still half-full. Stinking, moulding! The uninhabitable habitat of the mover of Her Majesty's mail—who never missed a train until that day...

Up on Central Avenue, a block and a half north of the CNR station, next door to the post office (with its **BUREAU D'POSTE** sign hanging askew) was the municipal office. Everybody in town called it the "mun-i-SIP-ul" office except for the principal of the school who always said "mu:-NISS-i-p'l" for some unknown reason; every-body else that is, except the u-sual and main and most important occupant of that office. He said "municipal" the way the principal did and for probably the same reason since they were the two most highly-educated men in town.

Ruler of that small-ly, almost-but-not-quite-royal realm was Jonothan R. Klinderquist, Bachelor of Commerce, University of Saskatchewan. Jonothan R. Klinderquist had a big job to do. Officially he looked after all the affairs of the town and of the municipality. Un-officially he looked after most of the businessmen's books, the school board's records, the farmers' income tax forms, and sometimes such quasi-legal matters as will-writing and marriage and divorce advice.

Funny in a way that he would look after marriage and divorce advice, because Mr. Klinderquist—which is what everybody--without excep-tion, called him—was a bachelor. A quiet man, temperate in his habits—

probably a teetotaler, but no one in town knew him well enough to be sure. He owned a two bedroom cottage on the north end of Central Avenue, just two or three minutes away from the municipal office by fast foot. That was his usual method of moving around town: a brisk walk like that of a man who knows where he is going and why. Mr. K's cottage was like something off a calendar advertising a Nova Scotia real estate firm: painted white, bright red shutters, a roof that glistened red with fresh paint

In Search of a Unicorn

every other spring, white picket fence, tulips first up each year and strawflowers staying brighter longer than any others in town. No one was quite sure what the inside of the house was like. The bright curtains on the windows were always closed; the doors always locked. The only hint of what was inside came from the sounds of beautiful music that floated out on the summer air. Violins mostly, but often full symphony orchestras or chamber groups. No one was even sure that the violin music always came from records. Or did Mr. Klinderquist play?

Once a week Jonothan R. Klinderquist drove to Saskatoon right after he closed the office. On those days—sometimes Tuesdays and sometimes Thursdays—he drove from his home on the north end of Central Avenue to his office in the middle of the next block. His shiny four-door was always a black one replaced each year at the Chevy dealer's down on Railway Street—but never a Chevy, an Oldsmobile ordered in special. As soon as he locked up the door on those weekly afternoons he got into his car and spun away like a devil possessed. It was out of keeping with his usually mild-mannered ways, the way he drove that car. Little children were warned to keep clear when they saw him take off for Saskatoon. Just like they were warned to stay at least a half a block away from Tinker the Clinker when he pushed his mail cart down to the station to meet the mail train or back to the post office after the train came.

Stay clear of Tinker the Clinker, Stay clear of Jonothan R. Klinderquist. And why not? Except for the United Church ministers who changed every two years and the school teachers who never stayed more than three years, everyone in town knew that Tinker the Clinker and Jonothan R. Klinderquist were brothers—twin brothers, at that.

The municipal office closed at 4:45 on the dot. Regardless of how busy the day had been or still was, regardless of how slack a season or dull the duties at 4:45 Mr. Klinderquist locked the door and went home. Or to Saskatoon if it was the day to go. By 4:48 he was around the block and crossing Central Avenue on his way to the edge of town. By 4:50 he was on the open road. Fortunately for him he did not have to cross the CNR tracks to get out of town. Fortunately, because the afternoon train stopped at the station at 4:48 and was usually still sitting around waiting for cream cans to be loaded or unloaded until 4:49 ;or 4:50 and sometimes even it was 5:05 or 5:10 before it pulled away. But the train never had to wait for the Clinker. He was always on time. It would have gone against his nature to be late for that train.

And it would have gone against Mr. Klinderquist's nature if he had had to sit at a crossing waiting for a train!

It was forty below that February afternoon that Tinker the Clinker was late. The 4:48 was on time and there were no cream cans to load or unload since the roads out into the farmlands had been blocked. The mail bags were thrown out and the train was ready to go by 4:49— except that Tinker wasn't there with the out-going mail. The postmaster had told Tinker to be fairly careful with the mail bag today. Somebody had mailed a little parcel through the slot and all over the parcel was marked **FRAGILE** and **VERY FRAGEL** and **REEL FRAGLE**. The postmaster had not seen who put the parcel in and there was no return address so he couldn't inquire just how careful the parcel needed to be handled. It looked like it could be a picture in a frame or something like that.

So Tinker was being careful with a mail bag containing a fragile parcel. But was that reason enough to miss the mail train?

At 4:48 Tinker the Clinker was pushing the cart south on Central Avenue, one block north from the CNR station when he slipped on the icy street. As he fell forward the pushcart containing Her Majesty's mail was propelled swiftly forward directly into the path of the sleek four-door Oldsmobile sedan driven by Jonothan R, Klinderquist.

Tinker missed the mail train that once—but it didn't matter, really. He retired a few weeks later to a whole new life and didn't need the pittance that the pushing brought him. Jonothan R. Klinderquist did make it to Saskatoon that evening, by air ambulance. But he didn't live through the night. Being the only living relative and Jonothan—of all people—having no will, Tinker moved into the little cottage on the north end of Central Avenue. He even kept up the garden year after year, and he played Jonothan's records so the neighbours could hear. He seemed like a new man. Some said it seemed to start when he slipped on the ice. In fact, some of the witnesses to the collision said that just before the explosion of the pushcart, Tinker had a strange look on his face.

APPENDIX F

An "Alphabet" of Churches of Christ

This list from a contributor who is unknown to me came via an internet posting quite some time ago. I do not know where some of these congregations are, but I have noted with an asterisk (*) those with whom I have worshipped or with whom I have had some sort of contact. For some I have added my comment(s) as to what I *think* is meant by their particular emphases.

1 AD 70's

> While most of us recognize that the church had its beginning on the Day of Pentecost, these brethren put an emphasis on AD 70 as the beginning date and they do not let anyone forget it! By the way: how many buildings have you seen (often, I have noticed, sitting obliquely on a corner lot!) with a

notation, sometimes engraved in stone, something like this:

Church of Christ Established AD 33

2* Black Obviously congregations of African-Americans, or sometimes simply Africans. In Jamaica on a couple of occasions, my wife and I had the experience of being the only two people of the two hundred in the congregation who were not black!

3 Chinese (members) again, obvious, but different from the next listing. These "members" were part of a non-Chinese community and had their own

congregation with services in English

4   Chinese language services
5   Deaf—congregations where most of the members are deaf and the services are conducted using sign language, though some have oral accompaniment.
6   Ecumenical (?)

>The question mark was not added by me—but it could have been because I have absolutely no idea what it means!
>
>If I were to hazard a guess it would be a congregation such as the one in St. Louis, Missouri, where Carl Ketcherside ministered.

7   French language services
8   Filipino membership

9   Indian membership

      I believe this grouping is American Indian, but I am aware of congregations in Canada with membership predominately First Nations (or aboriginal) members.

10   Korean membership

11   Laotian language services

12 *   Mutual edification (opposed to located preachers, institutions)

      Re-read chapter eleven for my comments on my pleasant experiences with this group. They also participated in the Family Camp at Macrorie, Saskatchewan, on at least one occasion—sending one of their preachers to teach. In the five or six years that Marie and I were winter-time only members of a Louisiana congregation, I was assigned one Sunday a month when I was charged with the "edifying".

13 No buildings (opposed to church ownership of buildings)

14 No separate classes, no located preachers—Similar to # 12, who also do not have classes. The little tots sit with all the old folks and hear the sermons—about sanctification and eschatology and all that!

15 No separate classes *with* located preachers—the difference between these and the ones above is obvious!

16 No separate classes with located preachers: girls speak until Christians (?) Now, to me, this category is

even more mysterious than # 6 (ecumenical) as I cannot imagine what it means—and I cannot trace the e-mail because it was so long ago.

17 Non-institutional and fairly straightforward in every way except for a belief that the church is not to run children's homes and schools, etc.

18 Non-institutional and women must wear head covers! I wonder if scarves are provided at the door for the unsuspecting? Once I visited a cathedral (Roman Catholic) during a summer holiday trip and I was provided with a wrap-around skirt to go over my

Tommy Downs

Bermuda shorts!

19. One cup only for the Lord's Supper; and there are no classes; and, there is no located preacher . Traveling evangelists (like the old-time Methodist circuit riders) are the speakers, usually.

20. One loaf (usually baked fresh by someone in the group) and divided as it is used—each person breaking off his own portion.

21. One loaf (likely freshly baked) and broken just before it is distributed

22. One cup, like # 19 except for having Bible classes

23 Prison church—obvious!
24 Pre-millennial, with located preacher. This category could actually be *any* of the others with the difference being only in the doctrine, not the practices.
25 Pre-millennial, but no located preacher (ditto!)
26 Russian language services
27 Spanish language services
28 Vietnamese membership

These are probably just a sample of the "kinds" of churches of Christ that exist! All truly churches, no doubt—but with variations that I believe are usually based on the ideas that somebody way back yonder had. I have often asked "why?" and many, many times, nobody knows why? Re-read Chapter Fourteen! Practically no one could tell me what made Free Methodists free. And the most odd thing to me is this: Only twenty-five years before my questioning them, Free Methodists did not use musical instruments in worship. Nobody I talked to knew that!

APPENDIX G

MEN WHO TRIED

to return to the Divine Plan

In Italy

Claudius of Turin (d. 839)
Jerome Savanarola (1452-1498)

In France

Peter of Bruys (d. 1126)
the Albigenses (1170)
the Waldensians (1170)

In England

Tommy Downs

William of Occam (1280-1349)
John Wycliff (1324-1384)
John Huss (1369-1415)

In Bohemia--Germany

JohnReuchlin (1455-1522)
 (Uncle of Melanchthon)

In Holland

Erasmus (1465-1536)

And who can overlook. . .

Martin Luther
Philip Melanchton (1497-1560)
Ulrich Zwingli (1484-1531)

==================================

And don't forget these two pioneers!
> *<u>All things not expressly authorized for worship are forbidden.</u>*

So said… John Calvin (1509-1564)
   . . . who also insisted upon. . .

In Search of a Unicorn

Absolute authority of Scripture

As did John Knox (1505-1572)
(Presbyterian Church of Scotland)

Don't forget *them*, but forget some of their teaching!

Five Basic Principles of "the Reformation":

1. The Bible, the word of God, the source of authority and the rule of faith and practice.

2. Religious principles and practices should be in harmony with man's rational nature

3. The universal priesthood of all believers--that religion is personal

4. Religion should be simple, inward, and spiritual, certainly not complicated, external and physical. Salvation by

faith only

5. They sought to establish "National Churches."

Denominational errors that arose:

1. Organization and government
2. Worship
3. Names
4. Creeds and confessions
5. Baptism
6. Subjects of baptism
7. Many matters of doctrine

In Europe: The Independents

1. James Haldane
2. Robert Haldane
3. John Glas
4. Robert Sandeman

5. Rowland Hill
6. Greville Ewing
7. John Walker 8. Alexander Carson

In America:

1. James O'Kelly
2. Rice Haggard
3. Elias Smith
4. Abner Jones
5. Barton W. Stone
6. Thomas Campbell
7. Alexander Campbell
8. Walter Scott
9. W. K. Pendleton
10. D. S. Burnet
11. Benjamin Franklin
12. Samuel Rogers
13. Tolbert Fanning

Tommy Downs

14. Jacob Creath, Jr.
15. "Raccoon" John Smith
16. Moses E. Lard
17. J. W. McGarvey

From "Restoration Principles" by Roy Deaver in *The Spiritual Sword*, Volume 6, Number 3 April 1975.

Appendix H

The Gospel According to Gimpy

The Reverend Ronald Richard Rockingham was facing a crisis. As a matter of fact he was facing three separate crises—three separate crises that were related, but related in such ways that he was unaware of those relationships.

The Reverend Ronald Richard Rockingham had only recently come to Regina—just last spring, actually. As rector of Condie Community Church he first faced up to what he considered the immediate crisis: getting a special sermon ready for Christmas. And in keeping with his determination to maintain a meaningful ministry, he.would not be satisfied with three points and a poem. He had to present the glories of God':s Gift in an atmosphere of awe.

As a clergyman in one of the three communions currently dedicated to creating "a new manifestation of Christ's Church in Canada," the Reverend Ronald Richard Rockingham faced crisis number two: he had to make his own position as clear as a prairie sky during a drought. He wanted everyone— everyone in his congregation, everyone in his denomination, and every one of the other ministers in the city—to know just where he stood on the matter of the churches' uniting.

Crisis number one and crisis number two had both developed slowly. By contrast, crisis number three came suddenly and absolutely without warning: Gimpy was gone!

Gimpy was Mrs. Ronald Richard Rockingham's cat. Cat is the zoologically accurate term, but really Gimpy wasn't much of a cat. Even as a kitten she wasn't much. Her near-nothingness was the direct result of her mother's negligence or shortsightedness. A wheat field on the Saskatchewan prairies in the spring is not such a bad site for a feline maternity ward under ordinary circumstances. But the last winter had kept these from being ordinary circumstances. winter had come early and the crops had been caught under a blanket of snow where they'd slept for months. When the warm spring sun dried the land enough to support the heavy machinery, the farmers hurried to take off one crop so they could get on with the work of putting in a new crop. And Gimpy's mother (no doubt of necessity) chose to have her litter of kittens and to leave them nestled neatly in her little straw-y spot—almost directly in the path of Mr. Haverstock's combine.

Mr. Haverstock was an elder in Condie Community Church. And he was an efficient elder. The

Reverend Ronald Richard Rockingham learned early to lean on Elder Haverstock. How do you keep the projector on when you turn the lights overhead off? Is it all right to throw away the ragged rug runner someone's Aunt Sally donated to the hallway of the rectory twenty years ago "in memoriam"? And what do we do about the water seeping into the basement?

Elder Haverstock usually had the answers when the Reverend came to call. And on that one particular spring harvesting day, he had more than answers; he had a problem--in fact he had a whole litter of problems! For along with kernels of wheat, Mr. Haverstock's combine had harvested a nest of kittens. One of them— and only one—was alive and kickin'. Just what does a kind-hearted, hard-working elder do with a maimed and mewing mass of new-born kitten?

Now Mr. Rockingham had a wife who was about as new to him as his prairie pastoral charge; and she was along on this trip, learning what she could of the ways of this new world around her. And Mrs. Rockingham had a heart of pure gold. Fool's gold, maybe it was in this case, but gold all the same! She decided the manse needed the pitter-patter of four little feet. So she decided to take the broken body of the com'-bined kitten home with her to nurse him back to his health.

Only two things were wrong with her philosophy: the pitter-patter turned out to be the pitter-patter-thump-slide of two and a half legs and a stump; and, he turned out to be a she.

Gimpy, as the game-legged cat came to be called, quickly became a regular member of the ministerial household. Everyone who met her agreed that Gimpy was a unique cat. Only Gimpy did not agree: That was because she did not know she was a cat. She considered herself on a par with people.

Mr. Rockingham managed to solve his first two problems by reading and research and reams of writing. He called into action all the forceful techniques he'd learned in seminary, especially from that last year's course in the communicative arts. Visual impact combined with the spoken word, participatory drama that creates an experience one can remember—these are the methods that will work. And all the time he was getting that special message put together Mrs. Rockingham interrupted only about two hundred twenty times to ask, "Do you suppose Gimpy could be....?"

On the Sunday morning before Christmas, the sanctuary of Condie Community Church was filled to capacity. Every word of the minister's message focussed eyes and attention on the almost-life-size nativity scene just to the right of the slightly off-centre pulpit. But the words did not just talk about the Baby of Bethlehem. The emphasis was on the One-ness of His church.

As he dramatically drew the solemn ceremony to its conclusion, the Reverend Ronald Richard Rockingham invited each member of the congregation to come forward, to gaze into the cradle, and to dedicate himself anew to the One-ness symbolized by the Baby there.

Poor Reverend Ronald Richard Rockingham! He could not understand the puzzled looks of his parading parishioners as they gazed into the cradle. He did not know why some who looked into the cradle then looked at him and shook their heads. Neither did he know what Gimpy knew: that straw in a wheatfield isn't nearly so soft as straw in a cradle, especially for three "brand-new kittens!

APPENDIX I

The Plan of Union of James O'Kelly

*In **Herald of Gospel Liberty** there is an extract from the writings of James O'Kelly under the title of "A Plan of Union Proposed," which is here in full as it shows his sentiments at the time:*

Should I, who talk of union, attempt to set the example, or lay down a plan, where should I begin?

I am acquainted with those of the Baptist order that my soul has fellowship with; but the door into that Church is water--and I cannot enter because of unbelief.

I am acquainted with some of the Presbyterian order, whom I love in the Lord. But before I can be a minister in that society, I must accede to, or acknowledge a book called "The Confession of Faith." This I cannot do, until I can believe that God eternally decreed some angels and men to eternal life, and the rest to
Eternal death--and this is unalterably fixed.

Should I propose to unite with my old family, the Methodists, to whom my attachment is greater than to any people in the world; notwithstanding their treatment to me: I could not be received, unless I could subject myself to a human head, and subscribe to an oppressive, and unscriptural form of government.

I would propose to promote Christian union by the following method: Let the Presbyterians lay aside the book called "The Confession of Faith." Which faith, is proposed to ministers before they are received; and instead thereof, present the Holy Bible to the minister who offers himself as a fellow laborer.

Let him be asked if he believes that all things requisite and necessary for the church to believe and obey, are already recorded by inspired men.

Let the Baptists open a more charitable door, and receive to their communion those of a Christian life and experience; and they themselves eat bread with their Father's children.

Let my offended brethren, the Methodists, lay aside their book of discipline, and abide by the government laid down by the apostles--seeing those rules of faith and practice were given from above.

And answer for doctrine, reproof, correction, instruction in righteousness; that the man of God may be perfect, thoroughly furnished unto all good works. II Tim. 3:10, 17

What more does the Church need,

than is above inserted?

Let their Episcopal dignity submit to Christ, who is the head and only head of his Church; and then we as brethren will walk together, and follow God as dear children.

O, how this would convince the world that we were true men, and not speculators--This would give satan an incurable wound; and make deism ashamed.

Again as each Church is called by a different name, suppose we dissolve those unscriptural names and for peace's sake call ourselves Christians? This would be-----"The Christian Church."

At present I can see no better method than what I here propose; but if any one can display a more scriptural method to promote union, for the Lord's sake let him show it.

All may see what I am at, I wish the divine Saviour to be the only head and governor of the Church, her law and center of union.

I wish all the faithful followers of our Lord to love one another with a pure heart fervently. Let them break down the middle wall of partition; and all break bread together.

Blessed will the eyes be that shall see that day. The shouts of the Christian Church will then be as terrible to the strong holds of satan, as the sound of the rams' horns was to Jericho.

Such a sacred plan as this, in my view would exclude boasting, God and his Christ would be exalted.

The followers of Christ were at the first called disciples, but at length they were called Christians. This was the new name which was spoken of by Isaiah, 62:2.

Those Christians compose the Christian Church, or the body of Christ. Brethren, if we are Christ's then are we Christians, from his authority, his name, and his divine nature.

This, if we would comply with, would cause the "residue of men to seek after the Lord; and all the gentiles upon whom my name is called, saith the Lord." Acts, 15:17.

The glorious temple erected by Solomon was walled, evacuated and utterly destroyed by the enemy: yea the very foundation rooted up. But the foundation of the Christian Church standeth sure, the gates of hell cannot prevail.

Therefore, all that we have to do, brethren, is to quit our babel, and as the soul of one man, strive in union to build the "Christian Church," with the golden doctrine of love and holiness, and the silver discipline of Christ's laws.

If a brother cannot say shibboleth as

plain as you, yet let him pass and smite him not. In matters not at all essential, we may bear and forbear, until God gives more light. Come, Christian, what sayest thou?

Let us not consider, every notion of the brain as the established article of our faith, or creed. Let not our reason be so imposed upon as to suffer our party zeal any longer to break the bands of Christian friendship.

You may observe the regular soldiers who are well instructed in the inhuman business of war, although they have their favorites, and mess together, but when the alarm of war is given, they behold the enemy approaching, they all unite under the same discipline, with life in hand:

They join in compact union, with one consent, in one common cause-- against the foe; they are then led on by their leaders as the captains of their salvation, and die by each other or gain the day.

But it is not so with us. We too, are soldiers against infernal spirits, and the power of wickedness, our weapons spiritual:

And we turn our swords against one another, and each party appears to be engaged in a separate cause, as if each name had a separate God. While all confess there is but one God, and one way to heaven.

I have observed that when a minister of righteousness delivers the doctrine of holiness and love, in doing this he must point out the errors existing among professors, there is some name generally offended.

After a person takes offense from something delivered from the pulpit, the remaining part of the sermon, however spiritual, is left to that offended brother.

But were we all of one name, errors could be exploded from the pulpit and the press, while the divine reproofs and corrections would give conviction, without offense. We could enjoy much more satisfaction of society in this world, and be better capacitated for the society above.

When souls are awakened by the voice of the Son of God through preaching, they then incline to forsake the foolish, and associate with people of good conversation.

They stand in the way, and ask for the road to life; each party casts out a clew and assures the strangers that their light is divine. The other name will warn the seekers against the errors of that people; for they build with "wood and stubble."

The inquirers stand astonished at the Christians, until they are tossed to and fro, like waves of the sea, and some have turned back, and walked no more with us.

O, why do we wander in paths of man's invention, or cleave to the example of modern churches; and why such violent attachment to names, seeing the royal standard is at hand?

Only unanimously agree that the Holy Jesus shall be the only head of his Church, and the only center of her union, and the one law-giver.

We then as brethren, and pastors after God's own hand, can preach Christ Jesus the Lord, and we will serve--for Jesus' sake.

[The preceding text was prepared in March 1996 by Jim McMillan (mcmillan@gala.lis.uiuc.edu) for the Stone-Campbell Restoration Movement Resources.]

APPENDIX J

The Promise

© 1968 Tommy Downs

Michael rested as best he could after Janet got the children off to school. He was unable to sleep soundly because he had to listen for the plane. Soon as the weather broke enough—if it broke enough—the six-passenger-when-packed Beaver would swoop down onto the lake ice beside the fish packing plant and Michael and five other men would overload the little plane for the ninety minute ride to La Ronge. They had been chosen to represent the other fishermen in the Lake Moustique settlement at a Saskatchewan government conference on conservation of natural resources and any father of twelve little Indians ought to be interested in conservation of natural resources. Finding enough fish and furs gets harder and harder year after year.

Janet walked over and sat down on the bed beside Michael. Tight in her fist she held three one dollar bills.

With what looked like reluctance she handed them to her tired husband.

"I've saved long time. You buy pretty cloth for dresses for our daughters—and something nice for our sons to share," she said. "And please, Michael, no whiskey. No beer, please."

Michael took the money his wife handed him, but he could not take the look she gave. He turned his head away with a jerk. "I try. I try. I try!" was all he could say.

But he could think and he could remember. In isolated Moustique, beer and whiskey didn't really bother Michael. They just didn't exist. Oh, sometimes a bottle or two were brought in and the white school teachers and the store managers probably had a good supply—but the five or six hundred native people of the area didn't have access to alcohol. That is, until they went to La Ronge or Buffalo or Prince Albert, or made it themselves. And when they did! Was it any wonder that the sad stories about Indians and firewater were so numerous?

Michael remembered and so did Janet, the time two summers ago, when he went to Buffalo. It was to a trappers' meeting. Fishing and trapping had been extra good. And there had been even more income from fighting forest fires and serving as a guide for fishermen. That Yankee fisherman had been especially generous. Michael had gone to Buffalo with about thirty dollars to spare. It was supposed to be used for a new gasoline lantern, or a parka and new boots. But Michael had spent it all—a little at a time over the four days, on liquor.

And three Christmases ago! How they'd like to forget that. All the money destined for Christmas gifts had somehow found its way into the cash registers of the hotel-keepers in Prince Albert—since hotels are the only places beer is sold in Saskatchewan! Michael was at an important conference where many experts were trying to decide some way to spark the economy in communities like Moustique. But Michael hadn't spent much time in the conference sessions after that first night in the city. And he had come home broke, in debt, and without any Christmas gifts. Once he sold his nice beaded jacket at half its value to pay for liquor…..and Janet had promptly made him another.

But Michael had promised Janet, "Never again." And he had made that promise in the presence of Father Rene! The Father had prayed for Michael. But he also had told Michael that it was mostly up to him —to Michael. He had to be strong enough to say "no" when someone suggested or offered a drink. And he had to use better judgment in spending his hard-earned money.

"Think, Michael, of those twelve children. They need you and all the living you can provide them. To lose you because of a knife-stab in a drunk brawl would be a real blow to them. But then, it wouldn't be much worse than having you around in a perpetual drunk, would it? Leave the stuff alone." Father Rene had said.

And Michael had left it alone. He didn't even taste the toddy the storekeeper offered him two years ago. And last summer he was guide for four weeks to a tourist who started guzzling in early morning, but Michael had not drunk a drop.

Of course, Michael hadn't been to Prince Albert in a long time either. Nor Buffalo. Nor La Ronge. But now he was about to go to La Ronge . . . for at least three days.

Maybe it's a good thing he had no

fish to sell. And maybe it was good the moose-hide jacket he wore these days wouldn't appeal to anybody—dirty, worn, blood-stained from the many animals he had killed for the family's food.

But Michael knew he had often left home penniless—and he had always managed somehow to buy liquor. And down deep inside Michael was frightened.

# # #

Overhead he heard the plane. Without even a good-bye the tired fisherman forgot his fatigue and left his wife standing at the doorway as he hurried to the lake. Janet called quietly after him, "Please, please."

As soon as the plane was in the air Michael began to doze. Somewhere between the first nod and the deep slumber he so much needed, he overheard the voices of the other men: ". . . can't wait! I can feel it tickling my throat now. Will the beer parlor be open when we get there? Will we get to stay at the hotel? Hope so. It's closer to the beer." Michael's fears became more and more real. But beautiful sleep made the fears go away for a while.

No one met the plane when it landed at La Ronge just before noon.

Tommy Downs

The men were on their own until suppertime—and that wasn't good.

As they walked along the long main street toward the hotel, Michael almost wished he'd slip on the icy street and break a leg. Then he could lie in the hospital a while and get rested up. No fish nets. No cutting holes in lake ice. No trap lines. No bills to pay with the new medical care scheme. And no chance to get drunk!

But then he thought of Janet and the kids. They'd be eating fish and bannock now, and for supper tonight—just fish, because the flour was almost gone. In his pocket, still tightly wadded were the three dollar bills. Two hundred yards ahead was the Co-op General Store and just beside it the liquor board store. A few yards beyond was the hotel—and its beer parlor.

Michael kept his promise—to himself, to Father Rene, to Janet and the kids. He passed by the liquor store and went into the Co-op. There he spent almost three hours trying to decide how to spend three dollars. When he left in mid-afternoon (mid-afternoon by the clock—almost night by the northern Saskatchewan sun!) he had bought several yards of yellow and blue cloth.

"These are the favourite colours of Moustique girls, these days," the store manager had said. "We've sold more yellow and blue than any other colours."

And for the boys Michael had bought a bag of plastic animals—nearly a hundred of them for less than a dollar. This was something they could divide and spend many hours with, when the blizzards kept them inside.

Michael felt good. And somehow he felt rested. Was it the sleep enjoyed on the plane? Or was it that a load had been lifted from his shoulders—

a load lifted when he spent Janet's dollars as Janet had asked? Whatever it was, he felt good.

As Michael walked out of the store, he met Nap, another fisherman from Moustique. Nap was already showing signs of too much time in the beer hall and Michael wondered why he was out walking around in the open now. He didn't wonder long. Nap said, "Michael, you're my wife's cousin. We good friends. Let's have a drink. You got money? I would buy you a drink, but I gotta wait and see a man. Don't have money right now. Buy me a drink, eh, Michael?"

"Nap, I gotta go to the hotel and get my room. I haven't checked in yet. And you know how Jim is. He wants all the paper work done before supper. And besides, Nap, I'm not drinking this trip."

Michael had said it. Someone had heard it. Now he had another reason to be afraid. He could not lose face.

Nap walked away muttering under his breath—swearing above his breath. Michael signed the register at the hotel. He was assigned a room with Father George and the two Chippewan delegates from Lac Laccine. Father George always came along because he was the only white man around who could speak English and Chip well enough to interpret. Perhaps on this trip he could serve another purpose, too. Perhaps his very presence would help Michael keep his promise—to Janet, to Father Rene, and to himself.

For the next three days Michael kept pretty close to his roommates—except for a few minutes the last afternoon when Father George and the Chips stopped in for a quick beer. Michael attended every session of the conference, too. He was the first in the hall every morning and the last one asking questions after the pow-wows at night. And through all this he didn't once take a drop of whiskey, wine nor beer. It hadn't been easy when practically everyone else was drinking. But Michael somehow felt it was a little easier the last day than the first.

Actually it ought to have been harder the last day. After the final session, before the planes left for all parts of the Northland, there was a lot of last minute celebrating. Some of these men wouldn't come back "outside" for many months. But when Michael climbed into the Beaver (up front by the pilot) for the trip to the settlement on the narrow strip of land between the Big and Little Moustique Lakes, he and the pilot were the only ones without beer-breaths. And Michael wasn't really sure about the pilot.

# # #

The weather looked good when they left La Ronge. True, it was colder—but seemed clear enough. It took a bit of shaking to break the plane's skis loose from the lake ice, but they lifted off in bright sun with plenty of daylight left for the ninety-minute flight to Moustique.

Tommy Downs

Forty minutes out of La Ronge a sudden mist closed around the little plane. From out of the northern nowhere it came . . . . and into the frozen somewhere the sun disappeared. The little plane flew on—as straight as the pilot could hold it. And he could only hope the mist would soon lift.

Michael clutched tightly the package of cloth and the bag of plastic animals. He thought of Janet and the kids, of Father Rene. He thought of his promise—the promise he had kept.

Three weeks later when the wreckage was found, the frozen

hands of Michael Runningbear still clutched to his stiff body a package of blue and yellow cloth and a bag of plastic animals.

APPENDIX K

The Silver Trombone

© 1964 Tommy Downs

I guess I knew I'd join the new band. After all, even when I was just a kid learning to walk they said I had "music in my bones." But I didn't tell anybody I wanted to join. There was a lot of talk about how the band would keep the kids off the street, give them something to do, and all that. And the Good Lord knows something needed doing. Like for example, that young Tom McDougall and three or four of his younger brothers running wild ever since their daddy died few years back. Seems they've broke into half the houses in town in the last few months. Went in ours while we were on holidays last summer. Just made a mess of things—never took nothing as we could figure. And so far they've never been caught at it— but we all know who's doing it.

Tommy Downs

Seems there's not a good streak in them anywhere. They need something to keep them busy. You know what they say about the idle brain, or is it idle hands?

Then, too, some have talked about how some of the little ones never get to take part in the Christmas concerts and variety nights and the like. And in our little prairie town these things ain't gone out of style like lots of places. The band would sort of give some of these a chance to show out.

The wife was the first one told me about the band. She's a school teacher and was all for it from the beginning. She wasn't so much for this nipping juvenile delinquency in the bud as she was just giving the kids a chance to learn music—though she thought stopping the delinquency was a good idea, mind you. She always was one to go in for this culture type things and this band idea was about the best chance likely to come our way. Seems a group of parents and a teacher or two had heard about a band teacher or bandmaster I guess you'd call him who was available one day a week—

out from the city. He had a reputation for showing up come hailstorm or prairie blizzard and his bands had won the ribbon in lots of exhibitions and concerts and so on. It did look like a pretty good thing for our town.

But what would people think of a forty-five-year-old elevator agent going down to the school every Thursday night with a bunch of kids? And I didn't hear of any other adults actually going down to join the band. I did talk to George Rush about it. I know George had played a clarinet in the band over at Sunflower years back. And somebody said Sam Sorrells over at the municipal office might join in "just to help out a while," according to him. He probably wanted to play in that band as much as I did but he wouldn't admit it either.

But I never had played anything but the radio—and the mischief sometimes, the wife says—so what would they do with an old codger like me? I just tried to forget the whole matter.

Then the kids got interested. My

kids, that is. The boy started it when he said big and plain at supper one night, "Daddy, do you think we can afford a trumpet for the band?" And I started to offering all the usual excuses: "Well, son, you know money don't grow on trees. And then there's the taxes . . . "

"Jim, now you just hold on." That was how my wife got into it. "I've been letting the housework go to pot these six years and standing on my feet all day and marking papers all night for something, you know. And one thing it's been for is so the kids can have some of the things you and I didn't have. And besides, "she sort of said under her breath, "I think I'd like to play in the band, too."

Well, young Jim just fairly beamed. Seems he already had his eight-year-old heart set on that trumpet—and Sharon, who just turned twelve, spoke up, too. "Oh, and then I can play the saxophone, Mother, just as we planned."

Just like we'd planned. Ain't that just like the women. The wife and kids had it all planned. We were all going to join the community band—

Mother on the glockenspiel, Jim on the trumpet, Sharon on the saxophone, and father had his choice: the bass drum or a trombone.

Well, I thought about that bass drum. Ought to be easy to learn, and too, the Board of Trade had bought some of the bigger instruments for the band to use and one they had was a bass drum. If I could get that, then there wouldn't be such an outlay of money.

So I told them I'd think it over and decide what I wanted to play, that is

In Search of a Unicorn

if I decided to join the band.

For the next two weeks, we had band three meals a day. And band in between! "Can I get a silver trumpet, Daddy?" "What's the difference between tenor and alto sax, Mother?" "I wonder if the glockenspiel gets heavy marching?"

Marching? Marching? I hadn't thought of that. Why, with that leg that's been stiff since World War II, how could I ever march? On the other hand maybe that's what I need to limber it up and keep the circulation good.

Tommy Downs

Two weeks to the day after the idea first popped up, I was doing some paper work just before I left the elevator to go home when Jake Turner came in. Jake is sort of a jack-of-all-trades. He sells a little insurance, manages the credit union part of the day and drives a school bus and things like that. He used to be our water man till the town water and sewer came in. Everybody likes Jake and he knows folks in town better than almost anybody, I guess.

"Jim," he says, "I'm sure glad you're going to join the band. We need some reliable, mature adults to make things go and to sort of keep things simmered down. It'll be a real encouragement to the kids, too."

Well, I hadn't told anybody what I'd decided so I was puzzled a little bit—and I just kind of stammered. "Yes," Jake went on, "You'll be worth a lot to that band. And I was wondering if you wouldn't like to help out in another little matter, too. You see, one reason for this band is to keep some of the boys out of trouble—so our committee is trying to get different men to help pay the

Tommy Downs

fees for some of the welfare kind of kids—you know, like the McDougalls. You see, young McDougall—Tom, it is—according to the teachers he is just vibrating with rhythm all the time. And he's applied to play the bass drum the Board of Trade gave the band. But he don't have the money for the lessons. Our instrument committee assigned him the drum in the hopes of getting some help for the lessons. How about it? We can count on you can't we?

I didn't really hear Jake after that.

Not a word after he said "McDougall". There went my bass drum, my easy learning. And to that no good McDougall kid!

I guess I would've swore a little about then if the telephone hadn't of rung. It was Sally at the central office telling me that the station agent had been trying to get me earlier. Seems he had a parcel for me and wanted me to get it before he locked up. So by the time I got through on the telephone Ihad cooled off enough to tell Jake I'd think about it.

"Well, that's all right, Jim," he said. "Take your time to think it over—but we're counting on you to do it. Your wife's already paid for you and her and the two kids' lessons for the next three months so you ought to be able to help us out with one of the McDougals. By the way, have you found a trombone, yet? Your wife said she was looking for second-hand instruments to cut down a little bit on the money outlay."

Trombone? My wife? Second-hand?

I was flabbergasted. All of this planning and scheming and

conniving going on behind my back. But shucks, I really did want to be in that band—and a trombone wouldn't cost too much money. Especially if I could find a secondhand one somewhere. I told Jake, "Sure! I'll pay for McDougall's lessons—now let's get out of here so I can pick up that parcel."

When I got the parcel home and opened it up I couldn't believe my eyes. My wife's aunt out in B.C. had sent me an old trombone! So old and tarnished it looked like it had been through a fire—or stored in a coal mine. You see, my very efficient wife remembered that old trombone in an attic years ago when she visited Aunt Sue—and now here it was, all for me. But could I ever get it silvery again?

It was a busy time at the elevator the next few days and when we showed up at the school house on Thursday night I surely felt sort of funny. It wasn't just that I was the only man in the band except for the United Church minister (and he's nothing much more than a kid himself) but I hadn't had time to polish that darn trombone! The wife and Jim and Sharon were all sporting brand new shiny music-makers and mine looked like it was just out of the charcoals. But it made sounds—and I have to admit it felt pretty good to be playing on it. Or trying to play I guess I should say. But it surprised me a whole lot how much even a forty-five-year-old can learn in one evening.

And that McDougall kid. Not only did he beat that bass drum like an old time professional, but he could fairly make the snare drums talk and

Tommy Downs

sing. I was kind of glad I was helping him. All in all, it was a good evening. Young Jim sort of topped it off as we were walking home from the school-house: "Dad," he said, "I'm sure glad you thought of us joining the band. I think this is going to be fun." And you know, I believed he was right.

Believed it until the next day, that is. Soon as my wife got home from school Friday she gave me a phone call. "Don't you have anything to do down there?" she wanted to know. Well, I'd been up to my ears in work till just before she called so I pretty well told her off. Actually all she wanted to find out was where I had put my trombone. She and the kids were going to polish it up a bit. Seems they'd been as embarrassed as I had been by having such a dirty instrument in the family.

But I had left my trombone in the dining room along with all the other instruments. And she couldn't find it. Believe me, I hurried home and we all looked but it just wasn't there. In fact it wasn't in the house anywhere. I just didn't know what to think. I tried to phone Jake but he hadn't come in off his bus route yet. I called Sam Sorrell up at the municipal office and told him what my trouble was. He said he'd try to get the Mounties over from Sunflower next morning and in the meantime we ought to just phone around and ask the neighbours about anybody that had been around during the day. Well, we did that. We kept Sally busy at the switchboard for most two hours, but nobody had seen slide not mouthpiece of my silver trombone.

In Search of a Unicorn

And old Mrs. Rivers next door said she'd been at the side window knitting all day and hadn't seen anybody near our place.

It sort of looked like my career as a trombone player had come to a quick ending—unless those Mounties could come up with some idea. Not much else to do except wait for Saturday morning to come. Pretty early Saturday morning there was a knock at the back door. We were still lying in bed: it's the wife's only day off, being a week-day teacher and a Sunday School teacher, too. I went to the door and standing there as big as you please, was Tom McDougall, with *my* trombone case in his hands. Before I could let out the outburst that was building up in me, he snapped the lid open and showed me the most beautiful, sparklingist silver trombone I ever laid eyes on.

"Mr. Turner told me that you were paying for my band lessons, so I figured the least I could do was shine up your trombone for you. I hope you like it,"

APPENDIX L

The Question-Mark Mind

© 1967 Tommy Downs

In my dreams one night

No! Dreams I cannot say—

Because mixed up and frightful

In a nightmarish way

I saw a little mauve man

In a spotted green suit—

Under better circumstances

Tommy Downs

He might have looked cute

But he tortured and tormented

And I really don't know why—

Until I was nearly demented

And almost wanted to cry

    To my ego he flattered

    About nothings he nattered

    Pseudo-philosophically he pattered

    My ramparts he battered

    My securities he tattered

    My convictions he scattered

    He destroyed all that mattered

Or so it seemed

After a long, long chase

Through time and through space

In Search of a Unicorn

He finally caught me

And tied me in a knot

Dropped me into a pot

Then danced with glee

How lucky you are

More fortunate by far

Than many a prince or a king

On you I'll bestow

(Though how you won't know)

A most remarkable thing

Then the little mauve man

In the spotted green suit

Took from his pocket

A long black flute

Tommy Downs

He fingered a tune

With a haunting refreain

Then he cut open my head

And took out my brain

I watched as he kneaded it

Like gooey bread dough

He punched and he pulled

To shape it just so

Like a seeded French loaf

He pulled it out long

And he sang as he worked it

A queer little song

From the West to the North

As the clock hands go

Ten, two, and four

In Search of a Unicorn

Now six o'clock, Whoa!

Turn straight South

Then jump and skip a bit

Land with a bang

And you've got it, that's it

Over and over and

Again for so long

The funny little man

Sang his funny little song

What was the meaning?

What was his pitch?

Why did he bother me?

This wizardly little witch?

Of a sudden he stopt

Tommy Downs

No more did he sing

But with malicious-like fervor

He did a horrible thing

Around the pot he laid a huge fire

And piled on the fuel

Higher and higher

Books, both true and fictionary

Encyclopedias, a dictionary,

Magazines and newspapers—

To these he touched his lighted tapers

And as the flames began to climb

I heard him chant "refine"

While my knees trembled like most men's

I heard his eerie prayer "Cleanse"

    To my ego he flattered

In Search of a Unicorn

    About nothings he nattered

    Pseudo-philosophically he pattered

    My ramparts he battered

    My securities he tattered

    My convictions he scattered

    He destroyed all that mattered

It seemed half the night

He kept me in a stew

Then he did a remarkable thing

That I never thought he'd do

He replaced my brain

And pulled me out of the pot

And he said, "You be thankful

For this new shape it's got

Tommy Downs

Because look everywhere

And you'll never find

A more useful tool

Than a question-mark mind!

APPENDIX M

Butcher

In late spring and early fall, I used to walk home from work. Going to work required some crucial timing. I could step on the bus outside my door and off in front of the school eight minutes later—twelve or fifteen on icy or blizzardish days. After a full day in a stuffy classroom I usually found a twenty-five minute walk in the fresh air invigorating. It's strange in a way, but I didn't use that twenty-five minutes to look at the spring scenery or new fall colours. Quite the contrary! I was almost like a blind man was I walked, except my eyes were usually glued to the latest issue of *Readers Digest* or *Canadian Short Story Magazine.* Twenty-five minutes of uninterrupted reading: a prize catch and I caught it as I walked home from work.

It usually took about ten minutes to clear the school yard *per se*, even longer if school had just dismissed. I usually left forty-five minutes or an hour after the kids had left, however; and on those days, of course, traffic across the sports field was lighter. Leaving the school grounds I walked briskly and briefly along a back-alley corridor that the city fathers had provided with a cement walk for just such use. Unfortunately for the neighbours to that corridor the city fathers had not been able to keep the school-oriented graffiti off the back-alley fence: "The principle is a fink." "Shakespear married an Avon lady" "Mr. Donnely can't teach Caesar cause Caesar is dead!" Etc. And far worse.

The half dozen or so houses I passed in front of—those whose back fences caught the brunt of the school-boys' felt-tipped pens—were like little mansions or mini-estates and were occupied by the upper-upper economic class of our city. Turning from the super-sophisticated

Tommy Downs

"road" that was the address of these upper-uppers, I walked along a crescent where all the homes seemed to house families with three or four or five pree-schoolers each. Mayabe some of them took refuge on the crescentsh' sidewalks rather than risk the heavier traffic on the nexert avenue where their multi0-family dwellings were. Whatever the reason, the sidewalks and street were little-peopled with dozens: walking, skipping rope, riding trikes, or stand or sitting and talking. I was only vaguely aware of these miniature multitudes as I walked and read.

Vaguely aware, yes. What was the little boy saying to me?

In Search of a Unicorn

"Are you a police?"

"What did you say?"

"Are you a police?"

"No."

"Oh."

I continued walking and reading completely unaware of the little boy at my heels. Unaware and then aware:

"Are you sure?"

"Did you say something to me?"

"Yeah. I said 'are you sure?'"

"Am I sure of what?"

"Are you sure you are not a police?"

"Oh, yes. I am sure."

Tommy Downs

Trying to become unaware again, I walked on. I didn't notice it at the time, but later I seemed to recall hearing him say "I sure wish you was."

I crossed over the busy thoroughfare that divides Regina in half, stopping at the dividing island because the **WALK** light really—for safety's sake—ought to say **RUN FAST!** As the cars rushed past in each direction there was no need for me to keep my nose in my magazine, so I thought. What had that little boy said to me? And more important: Why? What was it all about—if anything?

When the electronic helper hanging in the middle of the street changed his mind again and signalled me to move, I went back the way I had come! Back past the high-rises and the multi-families to the quiet crescent with the noisy kids. As I turned to the sidewalk where I had first been propositioned, I realized I didn't have even an inkling of an idea what the little by looked like!. I need not have worried. He found me—fast.

"You came back. You are a police."

"No, I'm not a policeman," I assured him. "I will help you, if you need me, though. Why did you want a policeman?"

My strangely-naïve, three-degreed academic mind had never been conditioned for the king of gross gore and horror I now heard.

Tommy Downs

"Somebody chopped up Suzy." Leg by leg, arm by arm, blood everywhere. He described how he had walked into his high-fenced back yard to discover Suzy, quite literally butchered it sounded like. Mother wasn't home, but Mother had warned him about worrying the neighbours about little things when she was not at home and after all Suzy was not very big, really: "not big as me!" So his television-trained, not quite-five-year-old mind now having logged some ten to twelve thousand hours in front of the one-eyed monster, he set out in search of the friendly neighbourhood policeman. But policemen do not walk residential beats in Regina. Only school teachers do!

In Search of a Unicorn

My little guide hopped astride a bright red three-wheeler and pulled a "U-ie" indicating, I assumed, that I should follow. He seemed to know exactly where he was going—and he also seemed to be a wayfarer in these parts—just a-passing through! Fully as far from where we first met as I had walked toward my home, we travelled in the opposite direction. Carefully scrutinizing the fronts of homes on a side street in the lower income housing section he informed me he had not lived here very long and he had to be sure we went to the right house. With a gleam of recognition and a beam of accomplishment bursting forth simultaneously, he led me around the house and up to the gate in the high board fence.

Opening the gate slowly, I walked in, scared. In a corner under a caragana hedge, I saw Suzy.

It's unbelievable how completely an angry Chihuahua can tear apart a life-sized rag doll: Leg by leg, arm by arm . .

Appendix N

The Macedonia Church

Located between Williamston and

Washington, North Carolina sitting on land given by my great, great, grandfather is the Macedonia church building. These minutes refer to the "Church of Christ"....

> Dating back to 1844, the Macedonia Church of Christ has worshipped in the original site, located eight miles south of Williamston on Federal Highway 17 and fourteen miles north of Washington. No original records are available, but a later minute book shows that Millie Woolard was received into the fellowship of the church some time prior to the year 1844. Other names are recorded, but no dates accompany them until 1854 when Jesse H. Woolard was baptized by Henry Dennis Cason who was believed to have been the first pastor of the Church; serving the years of 1840-1850. The first services were believed to have been held in what was called a community house. The church, while making progress during early years, seemed to have lapsed into a spiritual coma and almost passed out of existence. However, Josephus Latham came to its rescue and effected the reorganization of the church about 1855. Following this reorganization, John James Coltrain, the grandfather of Mrs. Susan F. Peel, ministered from 1855 to 1860.

... though the land was deeded to the "Macedonia Disciples of Christ trustees . . . to be owned by the church for the purpose of locating a building for the church membership . . ." The church's minutes show that it was a "Disciples" church.

> The church, with its 20 charter members, was enrolled with the State Disciples' Annual meeting on October 8, 18__ possibly as Woolard's School house as that was the first k___ name of the Church and its building. The name Macedonia was given in 1868. Just prior to this second period of inactivity, the late Kenneth Woolard promoted the construction of a building for the church in or about 1865. On March 6, 1868 Kenneth Woolard deeded to the Macedonia Disciples of Christ trustees one acre of land to be owned by the church for the purpose of locating a building for the church membership.

Since it was not until 1906 that the U.S. Census began to refer to churches that used musical instruments as "Christian" churches and those that did not as "Churches of Christ," it is really moot as to what the Macedonia church was called. Whatever its name, it has witnessed for the Lord throughout the area.

And throughout the words written about the Macedonia church when I see the names Wynn, Woolard, Coltrain, etc. I am reminded that my own grandfather was Kenneth Woolard Wynn. My mother's paternal ancestors were instrumental in the organization of this congregation, which I visited in the spring of 2008, and my newly-located cousin took me to the grave of *our* great, great grandfather.

When one sees these minutes of the Macedonia church written back in the 1840's, it is easy to see how God has preserved the church and his Holy Word through the years!

Appendix O

The Meaning of EIS

1. The way a Greek word is translated into English depends upon many variables. Here are some verses that translate "eis" in a different way from the way it is translated into English in Acts 2:38 in the Authorized (King James Version):

In Search of a Unicorn

Matt 2:11 And when they were come **into** the house, they saw the young child with Mary his mother, and fell down, and worshipped him: and when they had opened their treasures, they presented unto him gifts; gold, and frankincense, and myrrh.

Matt 4:24 And his fame went **throughout** all Syria: and they brought unto him all sick people that were taken with divers diseases and torments, and those which were possessed with devils, and those which were lunatick, and those that had the palsy; and he healed them.

Mark 3:29 But he that shall blaspheme **against** the Holy Ghost hath never forgiveness, but is in danger of eternal damnation:

Mark 4:7 And some fell **among** thorns, and the thorns grew up, and choked it, and it yielded no fruit.

John 6:17 And entered **into** a ship, and went over the sea toward Capernaum. And it was now dark, and Jesus was not come to them.

Acts 2:25 For David speaketh **concerning** him, I foresaw the Lord always before my face, for he is on my right hand, that I should not be moved:

Acts 22:30 On the morrow, because he would have

known the certainty wherefore he was accused of the Jews, he loosed him **from** his bands, and commanded the chief priests and all their council to appear, and brought Paul down, and set him before them.

Rom 1:11 For I long to see you, that I may impart **unto** you some spiritual gift, to the end ye may be established;

Rom 15:18 For I will not dare to speak **of** any of those things which Christ hath not wrought by me, to make the Gentiles obedient, by word and deed,

2 Cor 4:17 For our light affliction, which is but for a moment, worketh **for** us a far more exceeding and eternal weight of glory;

2 Cor 8:6 **Insomuch** that we desired Titus, that as he had begun, so he would also finish in you the same grace also.

Eph 1:14 Which is the earnest of our inheritance **until** the redemption of the purchased possession, unto the praise of his glory.

Philem 5 Hearing of thy love and faith, which thou hast **toward** the Lord Jesus, and toward all saints;

2. When a substitution is made in Acts 2:38 using the different renderings of "eis" some interesting results occur:

"Be baptized....**for** the remission of sins."

"Be baptized....**unto** the remission of sins."

"Be baptized....**against** the remission of sins."

"Be baptized....**into** the remission of sins."

"Be baptized....**until** the remission of sins."

"Be baptized....[to the] **end** [of] remission of sins"

"Be baptized....[to] **make** the remission of sins."

"Be baptized....**till** the remission of sins."

"Be baptized....**toward** the remission of sins."

"Be baptized....**concerning** the remission of sins."

Tommy Downs

"Be baptized....**throughout** the remission of sins."

"Be baptized....**among** the remission of sins."

"Be baptized....**before** the remission of sins."

"Be baptized....**insomuch** [as] the remission of sins."

(N.B. I realize that I have simply substituted words without regard to proper syntax.)

Amen and Amen!

Writing this book has been a challenge—and a pleasure! Every page brought back memories of people whom I have known and been blessed by. Trying to decide what to include and what to leave out is where the main challenges came. Many more people and places could have found their way here—but there is a limit as to what I could include. I hope that your understanding of what the church of Matthew 16:18 is, has been broadened and that your "family" may be bigger when you consider the many congregations around the world composed of individual Christians who are dedicated to serving the Lord Jesus.

When I have found myself in a place where I did not readily find a "church of Christ" I asked myself: "What did Paul do when he traveled to a new place?" My studies told me that he sought out people who were seeking truth. Go to them and worship with them and together you may find even more truth than you expected.

Marie and I spent a pleasant holiday on the islands of Saint Pierre and Miquelon, a department (province) of France just off the coast of Newfoundland—foggy, rainy, almost dreary, but pleasant. For worship with others, we had a choice: Jehovah's

Witnesses or the Roman Catholic Cathedral. We chose the cathedral. We were treated with respect and honour and dignity—and served communion as if we had been Catholics all our lives! And we sang gospel songs just like we had sung all our lives—only in French! *Amazing Grace, Just As I Am, Heavenly Sunlight, etc.* In Mexico we found *iglesias*—a lot like ecclesias-- filled with Christians, with whom we sang the same songs, *Amazing Grace, Just As I Am, Heavenly Sunlight, etc.*-- this time in Spanish. With these "strangers" we had a common bond: we had been baptized into Christ, and they were our brothers and sisters. What a joy to share such a heritage!

Acknowledgments

I would be remiss if I did not say "thank you" to Vern Munshaw who encouraged the launching of this project, to Heber Coltrain who was my guide "in Macedonia country and to my grandpas", to Linda Haddock who helped chase down a little unicorn, and to my wife Marie who put up with my little pet pony with just one horn for so many years.

www.ingramcontent.com/pod-product-compliance
Lightning Source LLC
Chambersburg PA
CBHW082032230426
43670CB00016B/2633